Activities to Undo Math Misconceptions

GRADES 3–5

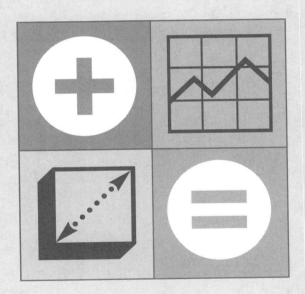

Honi J. Bamberger

Christine Oberdorf

HEINEMANN ✳ PORTSMOUTH, NH

Heinemann
361 Hanover Street
Portsmouth, NH 03801–3912
www.heinemann.com

Offices and agents throughout the world

The authors and publisher wish to thank those who have generously given permission to reprint borrowed material:

"Making a simple ruler" from *Teaching Student-Centered Mathematics: Grades 3–5* by John A. Van de Walle and LouAnn H. Lovin. Copyright © 2006. Published by Allyn & Bacon. Reprinted by permission of Pearson Education, Inc.

Library of Congress Cataloging-in-Publication Data
Bamberger, Honi Joyce.
  Activities to undo math misconceptions : grades 3–5 / Honi J. Bamberger, Christine Oberdorf.
    p. cm.
  ISBN-13: 978-0-325-02617-6
  ISBN-10: 0-325-02617-3
  1. Mathematics—Study and teaching (Elementary)—United States—Activity programs. 2. Mathematics—Study and teaching (Elementary)—United States. I. Oberdorf, Christine. II. Bamberger, Honi Joyce. Math misconceptions. III. Title.
  QA135.6 .B366 2010 Suppl. 2
  372.7—dc22   2010016303

Editor: Victoria Merecki
Production: Sonja S. Chapman & Elizabeth Valway
Cover design: Night & Day Design
Interior design: Jenny Jensen Greenleaf
Composition: Publishers' Design and Production Services, Inc.
Manufacturing: Steve Bernier

Printed in the United States of America on acid-free paper
14 13 12 11 10 VP 1 2 3 4 5

Contents

Acknowledgments

Writing books takes a discipline that goes above and beyond the call of duty, especially as we've juggled full-time jobs. We'd like to thank all of the editors at Heinemann whose assistance and patience allowed us to take the time we needed to "get it right." We also appreciate the sacrifices that our families (husbands, children, and even grandchildren) have made as we've taken time away from them to complete these books. Thank you, too, to Govans Elementary and to Oak View Elementary for allowing us to photograph children and activities for the books and for supporting us as we worked on them. Finally, a special thanks to the educators who inspire us and remind us to continue to learn as much as we can so we can inspire them.

Introduction

As experienced teachers who now spend our time working with both preservice and inservice teachers, we have talked at length about the challenges that students have with specific math content. Year after year, in one faculty room or another, teachers discuss first graders who still don't know how to count, third graders who still don't know how to add, and fifth graders who have no idea what a fraction is. How is it that no matter where we go there are second graders who don't "get" subtraction with renaming? And, why is it that fourth-grade students don't realize that a square is a special kind of rectangle? And, how is it possible that children in Alabama, New Jersey, Colorado, Pennsylvania, and Maryland (all places where we have worked) forget to say "fifteen" when they are counting by rote, by ones?

There had to be reasons why we kept seeing the same errors and misconceptions across states, in lots of classrooms, by many different students. So, nearly two years ago we began talking with teachers about the most common mistakes their students were making. We examined how relevant concepts and skills were taught, and we reviewed the mathematics programs that were being used. We found that, despite their best intentions, teachers often inadvertently contributed to the problems students were having. Early childhood educators, in their desire to nurture, support, and encourage young learners, could often be heard telling children, "Remember to always subtract the smaller number from the larger number." Or, when a student identifies a rhombus by calling it a "diamond," the teacher may tell the student what a good job he is doing with his shapes. As a result, students may not be learning the correct terminology of shapes or distinguishing numerals from digits. Young children don't really distinguish between digits, numerals, and numbers, so a first grader and second grader may think, when seeing $41 - 27$, that the "1" should be subtracted from the "7" because it's the smaller of the "numbers." So, in an effort to make a difficult procedure easier a teacher may say something that could contribute to a misconception that is difficult to change.

It certainly isn't just the things that educators say or don't say that can cause misconceptions. One need only look at the numerous posters and resource materials that can be bought for the early childhood and elementary classroom to see that there are many errors in these.

Let's take a look at posters, math-related literature, and resource books on geometry. Without naming names we frequently see "diamond" as the label for a rhombus, "oval" as the label for an ellipse, and "t-shaped polygons" (dodecagons) being called "crosses." We are even more concerned by the teacher resource materials and posters that provide students with "key words" to remember in order to solve addition, subtraction, multiplication, and division word problems. Posters may have the operation listed and then beneath it key words that students should be looking for so they know what to do to solve specific problems. Some curricula even have entire lessons written that tell teachers how to introduce and reinforce these "key words."

What makes this so bad? If the purpose of mathematics instruction is to teach for understanding, then looking for words and numerals, rather than the meaning behind the story, negates that purpose. And, since when does *altogether* only mean "add"? This story, "Altogether there are 23 children playing on the playground. Nine are girls and the rest are boys. How many boys are on the playground?" does not have students adding to find the answer.

▣ About This Book

Armed with resource books, posters, curricula, and statements made by well-meaning teachers, we looked at the error patterns and misconceptions that we were seeing in classroom after classroom. In this book, we address the most common errors we found in each of the five National Council of Teachers of Mathematics (NCTM) content strands: number and operations, algebra, geometry, measurement, and data analysis and probability. We offer you numerous instructional ideas for remediating a particular error, or for preventing a misconception from ever taking root. We also include black-line masters for nearly thirty activities and games that you can immediately incorporate into your classroom instruction. For each misconception, we also offer "Look Fors" to help guide your formative assessment during independent or small-group work. Finally, the accompanying CD-ROM includes editable versions of all of the black-line masters found in these pages. This allows you to customize our activities, either by differentiating the level of difficulty or making the situations more relevant to your particular students.

You will notice some misconceptions and error patterns that you might not have thought existed for students in grades 3–5. For example, in this book we have devoted an entire section to counting. But, if you look closer, you'll see the counting material deals with counting by fractions or decimals, a skill that many older students struggle with. Many fifth graders do not realize that there are an infinite quantity of numbers between .8 and .9, or that after .9 (when you are counting by tenths) that the next number will be

1.0. And there's another section in this book that deals with the meaning of addition and subtraction, since many children think that addition means "put together" and subtraction means "take away." Although these concepts are introduced in earlier grades, older students still have these misconceptions, and addressing them might help to eliminate them. We even have, in our measurement section, activities dealing with the telling of time, not just finding answers to elapsed-time problems. This intentional inclusion of practice with telling time on five and fifteen-minute intervals was done since so many third and fourth graders we've seen have difficulties with these skills.

▣ An Additional Resource

This activity book is a companion to our comprehensive resource book, *Math Misconceptions, PreK–Grade 5: From Misunderstanding to Deep Understanding*. In the resource book we share classroom vignettes and problem-based situations that give you additional insight into the misconception or error pattern that is being described. We also highlight relevant research and offer a range of instructional suggestions.

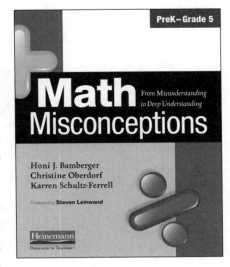

Our hope is that you will first read the resource book for a comprehensive discussion of the range of student misconceptions and the reasons behind them. You can then use this activity book to save yourself time in preparing some of the instructional ideas we discuss. However, if you choose to use only this activity book you will still gain useful insight into some of the more common mathematics errors and misconceptions and numerous ideas for addressing them.

Counting

 Misconception

Creating a student-generated pattern in the counting sequence to make sense of the existing sequence. Many students do not know how to count by numbers other than 1, 2, 5, and 10, beginning with those numbers. For example, if asked to count by fives starting with 3, they often count by threes or switch to counting by fives as if they began with 5 ("3, 5, 10, 15, 20, …").

What to Do

■ Ask students to skip-count from different numbers. If students always count by 2s beginning at 2, they memorize the "counting by 2s" sequence with little meaning attached. To support their skip-counting skills, expect them to begin counting from a variety of numbers. For example, beginning at 45, ask students to count by 2s: 45, 47, 49, and so on. Skip-count by 3s through 10s in this manner. Allow students to also practice skip counting by 11s, 12s, and up (including 25s and 50s) to facilitate number sense.

■ Read counting books (see page 2). After reading a book to students, challenge them to focus on an identified number from the book. For example, in *Moira's Birthday*, by Robert Munsch, 200 kids are invited to Moira's party. Students count to 200 in a variety of ways and record the ways on chart paper for sharing.

■ Support students in applying critical-thinking skills to the counting sequence by presenting number-logic riddles (see pages 3–6). When students are familiar with the format of the logic riddles, allow them to create riddles for classmates to solve. Encourage students to create number logic riddles for three-digit through seven-digit numbers, depending on the students' grade level.

■ Provide small groups of students with a large box of objects to count (for example, a box of craft sticks, connecting cubes, or paper clips). Challenge students to determine a way to count the objects in the box. Each group must have a different way of counting. When the task is complete, ask each group to present its counting strategy and to justify why the method is efficient.

■ Present opportunities for students to count both common and decimal fractions.

■ Provide experiences for students in which they place either common fractions or decimal fractions on a number line. For example, create a number line that is labeled 0 on the far left and 1 on the far right, and ask students to label the location for .250. This exercise also supports students' understanding of relative magnitude (the size relationship one number has with another).

Look Fors

As students work through these activities, check for the following understandings:

✔ Is the student able to count using a variety of strategies?

✔ Does the student use logical thinking skills effectively to solve riddles about counting?

✔ Do students use reasoning to justify why their method of counting is the most efficient for counting a large amount of objects?

Counting

Bibliography

This recommended list of engaging and interactive books helps children strengthen their counting skills and number sense. A brief description details the counting being reinforced.

Barry, David. 1994. *The Rajah's Rice, A Mathematical Folktale from India.* New York: W. H. Freeman. (Power of doubling.)

Buller, Jon. 1996. *Felix and the 400 Frogs.* New York: Random House. (Counting to 400 in a variety of ways.)

Harshman, Marc. 1993. *Only One.* New York: Dutton Children's Books. (Showing how single things are composed of different quantities, for example, three singers in a trio or a million stars in one sky. Challenge students to name other examples.)

Kuskin, Karla. 1982. *The Philharmonic Gets Dressed.* New York: HarperCollins. (Counting to 105 in a variety of ways.)

Munsch, Robert. 1994. *Moira's Birthday.* New York: Annick Press Ltd. (Counting to 200 in a variety of ways.)

Nolan, Helen. 1995. *How Much, How Many, How Far, How Heavy, How Long, How Tall Is 1000?* Buffalo, NY: Kids Can Press Ltd. (Absolute magnitude of numbers and exploring different ways of looking at 1,000. For example, 1,000 acorns in a pile versus 1,000 acorns that grow into 1,000 trees!)

Nolen, Jerdine. 1994. *Harvey Potter's Balloon Farm.* New York: Lothrop, Lee & Shepard Books. (Determining strategies for counting large groups of objects.)

Schwartz, David M. 1985. *How Much Is a Million?* New York: Mulberry Books. (Absolute magnitude of numbers.)

———. 1999. *On Beyond a Million, An Amazing Math Journey.* New York: Random House. (Counting by powers of 10 to google and beyond!)

Wells, Rosemary. 2000. *Emily's First 100 Days of Schools.* New York: Hyperion Books for Children. (Counting 1–100 with connections to everyday life.)

Number Logic Riddles

Begin first with riddles in which students are considering the numbers 1–9. This step enables them to become familiar with the vocabulary of logic. To help students think critically, ask questions similar to those modeled below.

Riddle #1:

- **The mystery number is after 5.** (Ask: Which numbers could the mystery number be? Which numbers could it not be? How do you know these numbers could not be the mystery number?)

- **The mystery number is before 8.** (Ask: Which numbers could it be? How do you know?)

- **The mystery number is between 6 and 8. What is the number?** (Explain how you know this is the mystery number.)

Riddle #2

- The mystery number is not after 7.

- The mystery number is between 2 and 7.

- It is a number before 5.

- The mystery number is the number of sides on a triangle.

For these riddles, provide each student with a counting chart (with numerals 1 through 25) and counters. Each time a clue is presented, ask a question that requires students to think critically and to justify their responses, as in Riddle #1.

Riddle #3:

- The mystery number is a 2-digit number.

- The mystery number is between 10 and 23.

- Both of the digits in the number are the same.

- The mystery number is after 20.

Riddle #4:

- The mystery number is a 1-digit number.

- The mystery number is an even number.

- It is between 3 and 9.

- The mystery number is the number of sides on 2 squares.

Number Logic Riddles 2

Provide each student with a counting chart (with numerals 1 through 50) and counters. Ask questions that promote students' critical-thinking skills.

Riddle #5:

- The mystery number is an odd number.

- It is a number smaller than the amount of cents in a quarter.

- The mystery number is between 12 and 16.

- It is the amount of cents in 3 nickels.

- What is the mystery number?

Riddle #6:

- The mystery number is an even number.

- It is a 2-digit number.

- When you begin at 3 and count by fives, you say this number.

- The mystery number is after 19 and before 50.

- When you add the 2 digits in the mystery number, you get a total of 11.

- What is the mystery number?

Riddle #7:

- The mystery number is counted after the number of days in the month of September.

- It is an odd number.

- The mystery number is between 34 and 44.

- It is the amount of cents in a quarter and a dime.

- What is the mystery number?

Riddle #8:

- The mystery number is before 25.

- It is an even number.

- The mystery number is between 3 and 18.

- When you count the number of sides on 4 trapezoids, you know the mystery number!

Addition and Subtraction Concepts

 ## Misconception

Thinking that addition always means "put together" or "join" and subtraction always means "take away" or "separate," making it difficult for students to solve a variety of addition and subtraction problem types.

What to Do

- Before using symbols, provide students with various materials that can be used to create part-whole representations of numbers (bicolored counters, connecting cubes, teddy bear counters, Cuisenaire® Rods).

- Use correct terminology for the addition and subtraction signs (+ plus) and (– minus).

- Provide students with opportunities to solve story problems that include all four problem types: join, separate, part-part-total, and compare.

- Provide students with some manipulative material to model the story problem that's been given, but have them also symbolically record what they've done.

- During a discussion about solutions to story problems, ask students to share the strategies they used to get their answers, reinforcing correct terminology.

- Use dominoes to have students generate part-whole addition number sentences.

- Use classroom routines to generate meaningful comparative subtraction problem solving. A "YES/NO" graph will provide daily comparisons.

- Provide students with opportunities to develop their own story problems.

Look Fors

As students work through these activities, check for the following understandings:

✔ When students share their equations, listen for correct use of "minus" and "plus."

✔ When students solve comparison subtraction story problems, look to see if students create two sets. Then look to see if they use an appropriate strategy to determine how many more or fewer one set is compared to the other.

✔ When students generate their own stories, look to see if they are developing a variety of problems based on the types and structures taught.

Spinning for Sums or Differences

See Appendix A for the spinners to be used with this activity.

Place a paper clip in the center of each spinner. Spin and record the values and figure out the sum or difference.

First Problem Spun _____ + _____ = _____	**Second Problem Spun** _____ – _____ = _____
Third Problem Spun _____ + _____ = _____	**Fourth Problem Spun** _____ – _____ = _____
Fifth Problem Spun _____ + _____ = _____	**Sixth Problem Spun** _____ – _____ = _____
Seventh Problem Spun _____ + _____ = _____	**Eighth Problem Spun** _____ – _____ = _____

Number and Operations: *Addition and Subtraction Concepts*

Name _____ Date _____

Using a Graph to Add and Subtract

Number of Letters in First Names of Students in Six Local Schools

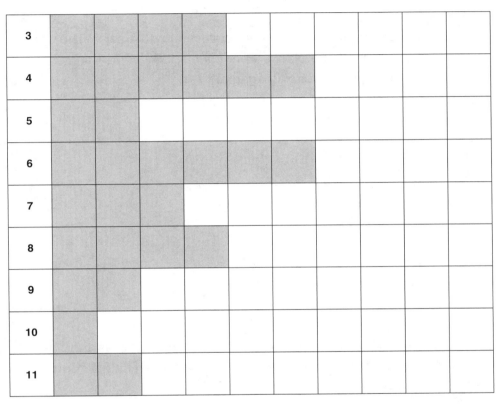

Key [   ] = 100 children

Use the data from the graph to represent addition and subtraction equations. Write the equation and then figure out the answers to each of the following questions:

1. How many more people have 6 letters than 5 letters? _____

2. How many people have 8 or 9 letters in their name? _____

3. How many more people have 4 letters than 7 letters? _____

4. How many people have 6, 4, or 8 letters in their name? _____

Addition and Subtraction Story Problems

Read both story problems. Decide on a strategy for getting your answer. Use this strategy and write what you did to get your answer.

The students at Patterson Elementary School were collecting bottle caps. Their goal was to collect 1,000,000. At the end of the year all of the caps were counted. Students had collected 63,478 bottle caps. How many more do they need to reach their goal?

Larry did not want his opponent to know how much money he had as they began the game of Monopoly®. After an hour of playing he had $3,400.00. He had spent half of his money on properties. How much money did he have to begin the game?

Place Value: Addition and Subtraction of Two-Digit Numerals

Misconception

When adding two-digit numbers students begin with the digits in the ones place and record the entire sum, then add the digits in the tens place and record this sum. When subtracting two-digit numbers students begin with the digits in the ones place and subtract the lesser digit from the greater digit, then go to the tens place and subtract the lesser digit from the greater digit.

What to Do

- Have students use their understanding of counting by tens and hundreds to group larger quantities, making it easier to count up or back to determine a sum or difference (see page 12).

- Have students use a five-hundreds chart to look for patterns and determine simple sums and differences by moving around the chart (256 + 200; 474 – 212).

- Use estimation activities so students get regular practice estimating quantities and then determining the actual amount by grouping by hundreds and tens to see how many.

- Have students share their solutions and the strategies that they used to get their answers. This allows for all students to see that there is more than one way to compute to find a sum or difference.

- Play games that require students to bundle, connect, or place objects together when there are ten of the object. Have students then record the quantity of hundreds, tens, and ones and the number that this represents.

- Give students a three-digit number and have them represent, either through modeling, pictures, or symbols, all of the ways to show the number using hundreds, tens, and ones only.

- Finally, have students use whatever strategy is *efficient* and *effective* in getting a sum or difference as long as it makes sense to them.

Look Fors

As students work through these activities, check for the following understandings:

✔ Do students understand the value of each digit rather than looking at the digit in isolation?

✔ Are students able to compose and decompose numbers?

✔ Do students see addition and subtraction as inverse operations?

Counting Up and Back to Get Sums and Differences

Use what you know about counting by tens (beginning with any number) or counting by hundreds (beginning with any number) to figure out the sum or difference of the following problems. Write what you are thinking—just like the example.

EXAMPLE: 456 – 210. *Think 456, 356, 256 (that's 200 less), 256, 246 (that's 10 less). 456 – 210 = 246.*

1.   879 – 420

2.   843 – 570

3.   908 – 432

4.   1280 – 470

Name _____ Date _____

There's More Than One Way to Add!

Look at the strategy Brenda used to solve this problem:

$245 + 359 \rightarrow 200 + 300 \rightarrow 500$
$40 + 50 \rightarrow 90 \rightarrow 5 + 9 \rightarrow 14$
$500 + 90 + 14 = 604$

Try to use the same strategy to solve the problems below:

1. $529 + 162 =$

2. $206 + 457 =$

3. $375 + 428 =$

4. $734 + 253 =$

Name _____ Date _____

The Choice Is Yours

Solve these problems in *any* way that works:

Problem	Estimate	Solve
784 – 269 =		
963 – 480 =		
1,128 – 304=		
604 – 299 =		
872 – 531 =		

Number and Operations: *Place Value: Addition and Subtraction of Two-Digit Numerals*

Multiplication and Division Concepts

Misconception

Applying addition and subtraction strategies erroneously to multiplication and division situations. For example, when multiplying 57×6, students round 57 to 60, calculate 60×6, and then subtract a single value of 3 to accommodate for the rounding, rather than 6 groups of 3.

What to Do

■ Number Lines

Rulers, yardsticks, and meter sticks can serve as number lines to model multiplication and division situations.

■ Equal Groupings (see page 16)

Making equal groups to model multiplication allows students to create equal sets and reinforces the notion that all sets are the same size. For the problem 57×6, when rounding 57 to 60 and then multiplying by 6, the students must understand that the readjustment of subtracting 3 applies to each of the six groups.

■ Partial Products and Partial Quotients (see page 17)

The partial products strategy emphasizes the importance of place value when multiplying whole numbers and provides an alternative algorithm that emphasizes the whole number rather than isolated digits within a number.

Partial Products:

57 equals 50 plus 7

$$\begin{array}{ccc} & \times 6 & \times 6 & \times 6 \\ \hline & & 300 & + 42 = 342 \end{array}$$

The same can be done by pulling out equal groups for division and then finding the total quotient by adding all of the partials.

Partial Quotients:

$$\begin{array}{ll} 6\overline{)342} & 6 \times \mathbf{50} = 300 \\ \underline{-60} & 6 \times \mathbf{7} = 42 \\ 12 & 50 + 7 = \mathbf{57} \end{array}$$

■ Area Model of Multiplication (see page 18)

By using an area model in conjunction with a rounding strategy, students see the value of the rounded product and how it compares to the actual product. This representation displays why an adjustment is necessary and how much of an adjustment should be made to the rounded product.

Look Fors

As students work through these activities, check for the following understandings:

✔ All groups must be the same size when solving multiplication and division problems.

✔ Adjustments made to any one group (for ease of computation) must also be applied to all groups when solving multiplication and division problems.

Equal Groupings

See Appendix B for the spinner to be used with this activity.

Spin the spinner and toss a 1–6 number cube. The spinner tells you the size of each group and the cube tells you the number of groups. Draw a picture of the multiplication problem and show the strategy you used to solve the equation.

Play again. This time create a division problem. The spinner represents the dividend and the number cube represents the divisor.

What if the spinner included a 10? What would your answers look like for multiplication and division?

Number and Operations: *Multiplication and Division Concepts*

May be copied for classroom use. © 2010 by Honi J. Bamberger and Christine Oberdorf from *Activities to Undo Math Misconceptions, Grades 3–5* (Heinemann: Portsmouth, NH).

Name _____ Date _____

Finding Partial Quotients

When dividing a number into groups, it is not always necessary to divide the entire quantity at one time. You may choose to take out chunks of the number until the entire amount is divided. See the following example and "think aloud" notes.

$6\overline{)57}$

I know 10 is too big because $6 \times 10 = 60$.

_____

$6\overline{)57}$ 5
$-\,30$
   27

I can take out 5 groups of 6 because I know that is 30. I still have 27 left.

_____

$6\overline{)57}$ 5
$-\,30$ 4
   27
$-\,24$
    3

I will take out 4 more sets of 6 because $6 \times 4 = 24$ and I have 27.

_____

$6\overline{)57}$ 5
$-\,30$ +4
   27   9
$-\,24$
    3

Five and 4 gives me 9, so the answer is 9. There are 3 left, not enough to put another in each group.

$57 \div 6 = 9$, remainder 3

Create your own division problem to solve using partial quotients.

....

Number and Operations: *Multiplication and Division Concepts*

Name _____ Date _____

Area Model

18 is close to **20**

Rounding is a strategy often used to estimate and find products.

1. Round the multiplicand to the nearest 10.

2. Multiply the rounded multiplicand by the multiplier. On centimeter grid paper, shade the array to represent the estimated product.

3. Place base-ten blocks over the shaded area to find the actual product of the original expression. Use the largest and fewest blocks possible to cover the array.

4. Compare the estimated product with the actual product and explain the difference.

5. Name the array that represents the difference.

<u>Example</u>
18 × 7
18 is rounded to 20.
20 times 7 is shaded on the grid.
18 × 7 is displayed using base-ten blocks over the shaded portion of the grid.
Compare the difference between the estimate and the actual product.
Label the array of the difference.

18 × 7   20 × 7

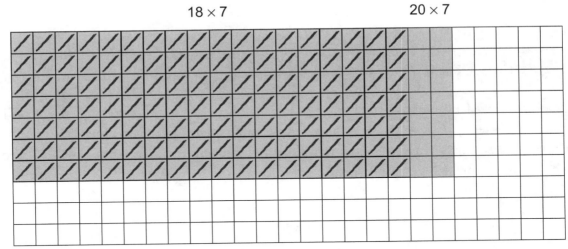

The differences is 2 × 7 or 14.

What if the estimated product is less than the actual product? How would you adjust your estimate?

Multiplication: Two-Digit by Two-Digit

Misconception

Treating each digit of each factor as a single-digit numeral and consequently performing the algorithm for multiplication incorrectly because students randomly multiply single digits rather than consider the value of the whole number. In the problem below, the student multiplied 7 ones by 4 ones and recorded the 8 for 28. She then multiplied 2 tens times 4 ones and recorded the 8 in the tens place. She failed to recognize the value of 30 in 34 and the 2 tens in $7 \times 4 = 28$.

$$\begin{array}{r} 34 \\ \times 27 \\ \hline 88 \end{array}$$

What to Do

■ Before doing any computation have students estimate the product, based on the numbers in the expression. Any strategy (front-end, rounding, compatible numbers) can be used to determine this estimate.

■ Have students "expand" the factors of the multiplication expression. For example:

$34 \times 27 = (30 + 4) \times (20 + 7)$ or
$\qquad = (34 \times 20) + (34 \times 7)$ or
$\qquad = (30 \times 27) + (4 \times 27)$

Perhaps try all three ways to see if different results will be achieved.

• Build the array that matches the expression using either base-ten blocks or centimeter grid paper.

• Dissect the array by comparing it with the expanded form of the expression so students can see all of the different factors and partial products that will form from a two-digit by two-digit expression.

• If it's the first expanded form that's used, have students explain where the 30×20 part of the array can be found and label this as $30 \times 20 = 600$. Then have the student explain where the $4 \times 20 = 80$ part of the array can be found and label this. Do this for the 30×7 part and the 4×7 part.

■ Try another expression and work on it as a whole group before having students do this either independently or with a partner.

Look For

✔ As students work through the activities that follow, look to see if they are using a strategy that is both *efficient* and *effective*. Also, be sure to ask students to explain to you how they know that they have used all of the digits in each of the factors as they've multiplied.

34

27

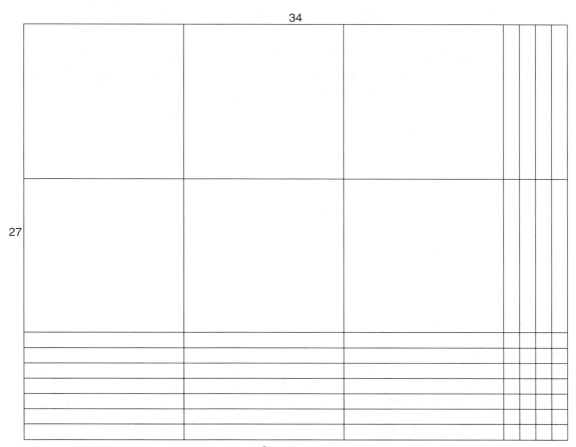

Sample array

The Choral Assembly

Use words, pictures, and symbols to solve the following story problem.

The school cafeteria is being set up for the choral assembly to be performed on Monday night. Eighteen chairs are in each of 21 rows. How many people will have seats at this performance?

The chorus is planning to take their show on the road by performing at a state competition later this year. They are selling candy bars to raise money for their trip. Fifty-two cases of 36 bars were ordered. How many candy bars are they planning to sell?

Number and Operations: *Multiplication: Two-Digit by Two-Digit*

Name _____ Date _____

Figure Out the Expression

Here is the product: 798.

Here is the array representing the expression:

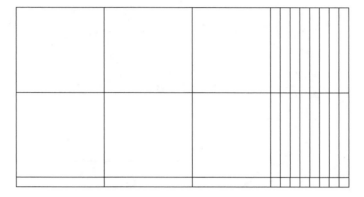

What is the expression that matches this representation? _____

Explain how you know that this is the correct expression.

Different Ways to Multiply

Here is a *different way* that students sometimes multiply 2-digit by 2-digit problems. See if this method make sense to you. Then use this method to solve problems 1 and 2.

$43 \times 62 = 2,666$

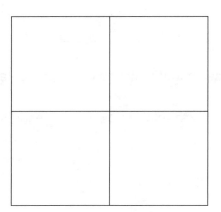

	40 + 3	
60	2,400	180
+		
2	80	6

```
 2,400
   180
    80
+    6
 2,666
```

PROBLEM 1

$76 \times 19 =$

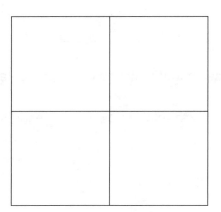

PROBLEM 2

$56 \times 47 =$

Using Different Strategies to Multiply Two-Digit Numbers

There are many ways that you can multiply and still get the correct product. One strategy is to halve the first factor and double the second factor until you get all the way down to 1 times the number. Once you have 1 times the number, you will have the product. Check it out!

Let's multiply 18×24.

Halve the 18 so it's 9 and double the 24 so it's 48. Use a calculator to see if 18×24 has the same product as 9×48. Cool, huh? OK, keep going—half of 9 (hmmm, that's a mixed number, isn't it?). Let's first take 1 group of 48 away and hold it to the side so we now have 8 groups of 48. Half of 8 is 4 and double 48 is 96. $4 \times 96 + 48$ (that's the group you took away) should be the same product as 18×24. Is it? Now take half of 4 and that's 2 and double 96 and that's 192. And, take half of 2 and that's 1 and double 192 and that's 384. That should be the product—but remember that you have to add that group of 48 since you took it out earlier.

18×24
9×48 1 group of 48
4×96
2×192
1×384
$384 + 48 = 432$ (which is the product of 18×24)

This procedure is called the "Russian Peasant Method of Multiplication." Use this procedure to figure out the product of the following expressions:

12 × 54	36 × 16
26 × 17	40 × 63

Number and Operations: *Multiplication: Two-Digit by Two-Digit*

Division Algorithm

 ## Misconception

When using the traditional division algorithm to divide, students treat each digit in the dividend in isolation to the entire numeral.

What to Do

- Encourage students to estimate the quotient using their mental multiplication skills so they have a sense of whether their answer is reasonable.

- Before using symbols, provide students with a story problem that is meaningful to them.

- Provide students with some manipulative material to model the story that's been given, but have them also symbolically record what they've done.

- Ask students to share the strategies they used and discuss whether their answers make sense.

- "Try out" someone's procedure that is both *efficient* and *effective* to see if other students are able to use the same strategy.

- Use number-sense activities to foster mental computation and an understanding of how to use multiples of ten to arrive at answers.

- Look at ways to adjust numbers to make them easier to use for computing (see page 30).

Look Fors

As students work through these activities, check for the following understandings:

✔ Check to see if students have a procedure that will always work.

✔ As students use their own division algorithm, make sure that they can articulate why it works and how they know their answer makes sense.

Sharing Candies

You may use whatever you like to solve this story problem. But once solved, you need to record, symbolically, what you did to get the answer.

Nina figured out that her candy bag held 327 candies. She and her 4 friends would be sharing the candy fairly. How many candies would each person get and will there be any left over? If there are leftover candies, what should be done with them?

Number and Operations: *Division Algorithm*

Name _____ Date _____

Estimating Quotients

Look at the following division expressions and choose the estimate that makes the most sense. Explain your thinking in selecting this estimate.

458 ÷ 6 =   a. 70   b. 75   c. 65   d. 60

_____

_____

_____

_____

726 ÷ 4 =   a. 200   b. 180   c. 150   d. 175

_____

_____

_____

_____

695 ÷ 5 =   a. 125   b. 130   c. 100   d. 135

_____

_____

_____

_____

Keeping the Balance, But Making It Easier to Divide

For each expression you need to decide what you will do to make it easier to determine the exact quotient. Write down what you're doing (including the "new" expression) and then figure out the quotient.

$1430 ÷ 5 =$

_____

$2,531 ÷ 25 =$

_____

$312 ÷ 2 =$

_____

$854 ÷ 20 =$

_____

$381 ÷ 5 =$

_____

Fractions

 Misconception

Overgeneralizing the meaning of fractions due to limited experiences with dividing regions and sets into fair shares. For example, students identify a half as one of two parts, rather than one of two equal parts.

What to Do

■ Provide students multiple opportunities to share a variety of objects, which supports them in thinking more flexibly about fractions. Present nontraditional shapes for students to divide (for example, a triangle).

■ Involve students in discussions following their experiences in working with fractions. Reinforce fraction vocabulary and talk about fractional parts first before involving any fraction symbolism. Then expect students to explain what the symbolic representation means.

■ Encourage students to "fair share" a grid outline in different ways (see page 32). For example, on a 4 × 6 grid of squares, the grid can be divided into halves by drawing a line through the middle either horizontally or vertically; the number of boxes (24) can also be divided into 2 areas of 12 in a variety of ways. Use the same grids and ask students to divide them into 4 equal parts in different ways.

■ Provide opportunities for students to solve word problems involving both area and set models of fractions.

■ Provide students with opportunities to develop understandings about fractional concepts in a variety of real-life connections. Reach beyond the pizza connection!

■ Present sharing problems that include the "set" model of fractions to help students establish important connections with many real-world uses of fractions.

■ Provide opportunities for students to explore fractions such as sixths or eighths (see page 33). Their understandings about "halving" will help them as they work with a variety of fractions.

■ Count fractional parts with students so they see how multiple parts compare to the whole. A "Days of the Week" fraction bar is included on page 34. This fraction bar can be added to students' calendar routine. For example, Sunday would be counted as one-seventh, Monday two-sevenths, and Tuesday three-sevenths. The fraction bar can also be used in problem-solving situations. For example, "If three-sevenths of the week has passed, what part of the week remains?" (four-sevenths: Wednesday, Thursday, Friday, Saturday).

Look Fors

As students work through these activities, check for the following understandings:

✔ Are students able to fairly share an area in different ways?

✔ Are students able to divide a variety of shapes or objects accurately?

✔ Are students able to represent fractional parts in various nontraditional ways?

Name _____ Date _____

Halves and More Halves

How many ways can you divide the grids below into halves?

Show your work on the grids below.

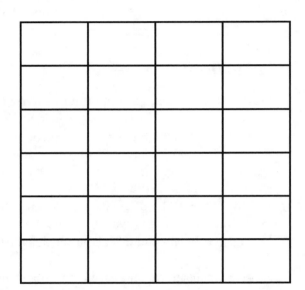

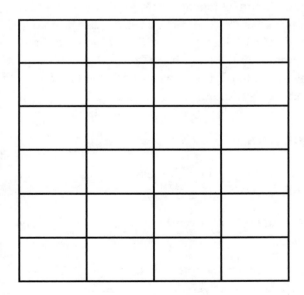

Number and Operations: *Fractions*

Paper Folding

Have students cut out the triangle below. Provide oral directions for folding the triangle into halves and then eighths:

1. Fold the triangle into half by folding the left vertex (at base of triangle) over to meet the right vertex.

2. Fold in this manner 2 more times.

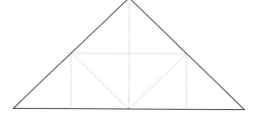

Ask students to label each eighth using fractional notation. Let students count the fractional parts in the triangle (one-eighth, two-eighths, three-eighths, four-eighths, and so on).

Engage older students to create story problems using their triangle. For example, five-eighths of a triangle is shaded, and the question could be, "Shade one-eighth more of the triangle. What is the fraction that tells how much of the triangle is now shaded?"

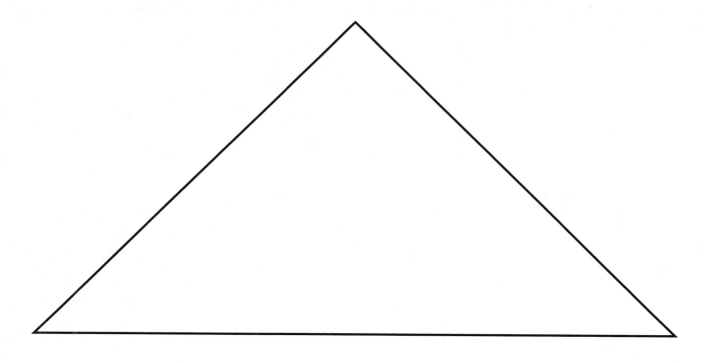

Days of the Week

1/7	1/7	1/7	1/7	1/7	1/7	1/7
Sunday	Monday	Tuesday	Wednesday	Thursday	Friday	Saturday

The "Days of the Week" fraction bar shows the passing of the week (enlarge if needed) and can be placed on your calendar board. When counting the fractional parts of the week, for example, if the day is Tuesday, begin counting on Sunday (one-seventh), Monday (two-sevenths), and, finally, Tuesday is counted as three-sevenths.

(Cut on all solid lines on the top half. The bottom half is only cut out on outside solid lines. The solid lines separating days should not be cut. The dashed line is folded over to cover days.)

Adding and Subtracting Fractions

➕ Misconception

Applying procedures for addition and subtraction of whole numbers to addition and subtraction of fractions. For example, when students add common fractions with like denominators, they add the numerators together and then add the denominators together. When students subtract common fractions with like denominators, they subtract the numerators and then subtract the denominators.

What to Do

- Allow students to create their own materials or draw their own representations when adding and subtracting fractions.

- Introduce activities in which students count by fractions. Begin by using manipulatives with which children are already familiar—pattern blocks, for example.

- Have students use fraction pieces to count by halves, thirds, fourths, sixths, eighths, and even twelfths. If they get good at this, ask them to combine strips from their kit: "If you have 5 of the one-twelfth pieces and you add 2 more one-twelfth pieces, what fraction will you have?" Be careful to ask the right questions. The answer to "How many pieces do you now have?" is 7, not the answer you want.

- Introduce story problems that reinforce what it means to add and subtract fractions. Don't have students record the equation until they have shared their strategies for getting their answers. Once students have been introduced to a number of examples ask, "What do you notice about how fractions are added or subtracted when the denominators are the same?" Reinforce that if you have eighths and add more eighths, you'll end up with even more eighths. It just makes sense.

- Give students opportunities to compare fractions (see page 37). This opportunity to visualize the value of a fraction will help in making sense of the computation when finding sums and differences.

- Use the number line to represent fractions. The number line is an effective tool for comparing the magnitude of fractions as well as adding and subtracting fractions with like denominators.

- Reveal patterns on the multiplication chart as an example of equivalent fractions (see page 38). This activity will serve as a precursor to students understanding how to name equivalent forms of a fractions when adding and subtracting fractions with unlike denominators.

Look Fors

As students work through these activities, check for the following understandings:

✔ The denominator names the total number of pieces needed to form the whole.

✔ The numerator indicates a specific number of pieces of the unit.

✔ While the numerator changes when adding and subtracting fractions with like denominators, the denominator remains the same in the sum or difference.

Apple Surprise

Shelby and her brother are making an apple dessert. The recipe calls for $4\frac{1}{2}$ cups of flour. Shelby can only find the $\frac{1}{4}$-cup measuring cup. Help Shelby and her brother figure out how many $\frac{1}{4}$ cups they need to reach $4\frac{1}{2}$ cups of flour.

Show your thinking with words, pictures, or numbers.

May be copied for classroom use. © 2010 by Honi J. Bamberger and Christine Oberdorf from *Activities to Undo Math Misconceptions, Grades 3–5* (Heinemann: Portsmouth, NH).

Number and Operations: *Adding and Subtracting Fractions*

Name _____ Date _____

More or Less Cards

For Card E and Card F, fill in your own fractions to compare. Then cut out the task cards, shuffle them, and place them facedown. Draw a task card and a representation (picture, number line, and so on) to justify which is more and which is less. Explain how you know.

For an extra challenge, determine how much more or how much less.

Card A

Which is more?
How do you know?

$\dfrac{3}{4}$ $\dfrac{2}{3}$

Card B

Which is less?
How do you know?

$\dfrac{4}{6}$ $\dfrac{5}{10}$

Card C

Which is more?
How do you know?

$\dfrac{4}{6}$ $\dfrac{5}{10}$

Card D

Which is less?
How do you know?

$\dfrac{5}{8}$ $\dfrac{6}{9}$

Card E

Which is more?
How do you know?

Card F

Which is less?
How do you know?

Soooo Many Equivalent Fractions

Read 2 adjacent rows of numerals as fractions. These fractions are equivalent.

For example, $\frac{1}{2} = \frac{2}{4} = \frac{3}{6} = \frac{4}{8} = \frac{5}{10} = \frac{6}{12} = \frac{7}{14} = \frac{8}{16} = \frac{9}{18}$

+	1	2	3	4	5	6	7	8	9
1	1	2	3	4	5	6	7	8	9
2	2	4	6	8	10	12	14	16	18
3	3	6	9	12	15	18	21	24	27
4	4	8	12	16	20	24	28	32	36
5	5	10	15	20	25	30	35	40	45
6	6	12	18	24	30	36	42	48	54
7	7	14	21	28	35	42	49	56	63
8	8	16	24	32	40	48	56	64	72
9	9	18	27	36	45	54	63	72	81

1. List at least 4 fractions equivalent to $\frac{2}{3}$.

2. How could you find several fractions equivalent to $\frac{1}{4}$ using the chart above?

3. How could you use the chart to help add or subtract fractions with unlike denominators?

4. Why does this work? What is really happening as you travel across the multiplication chart to form equivalent fractions?

Number and Operations: *Adding and Subtracting Fractions*

Representing Decimals

Applying whole-number concepts to decimal fractions; for example, students ordering decimals by the number of digits rather than the value. Students may also align digits rather than decimal points when adding and subtracting decimals.

What to Do

- Correctly name the decimal fraction (see page 40). When a decimal fraction is read correctly, the name reinforces the place value of each digit. Prevent students from getting into the habit of saying "six point three" rather than "six and three-tenths" when reading a decimal fraction.

- Use a variety of concrete models to represent decimal fractions. Students need multiple representations for decimal fractions. Such models include base-ten materials, money, meter sticks, and Digi-Blocks®.

- Provide opportunities to reinforce place value. With experience, students will recognize the relationship among adjacent values and see that moving to the left by one digit means *ten times larger*, and moving to the right denotes *one-tenth of the value*. Additionally, students must have opportunities to recognize that a value can be named using different units. For example: 45.3 may represent four tens, five ones, and three-tenths, or forty-five ones and three-tenths, or four hundred fifty-three-tenths.

Look Fors

As students work through these activities, check for the following understandings:

✔ Students verbalize the decimal fraction correctly.

✔ Students are able to state the value of a specific digit within a decimal fraction.

✔ Students can construct more than one visual representation for a decimal number.

Name _____ Date _____

Decimal Fractions

Complete the chart below for each decimal fraction. The 10 × 10 grid has a value of 1 whole.

Decimal Fraction	Word Form	Representation (10 × 10 grid has a value of 1 whole)	Value Ranking Least, Middle, Greatest
0.4			
0.23			
1.0			

On the back, explain how you decided on your ranking.

Also, show the **sum of all 3 values** and **the difference between any 2 values**.

Number and Operations: *Representing Decimals*

Name _____   Date _____

Racing to 4!

On your turn, roll the 0–9 white die (tenths) and the 0–9 color die (hundredths). Shade the total amount rolled. Complete the t-chart after each turn to show your progress. The first player to reach at least 4 wholes wins!

Value Rolled	Total

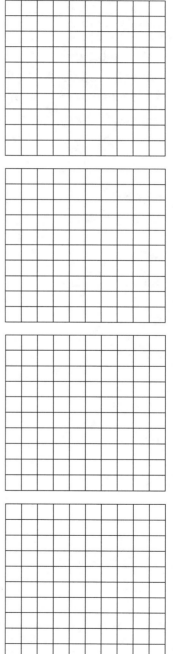

Name _____ Date _____

Pathways

Materials: Game board; marker for each player (up to three players); and spinner (see Appendix C).

All players begin in the center at START. Taking turns, each player spins the spinner and moves his or her marker in the direction indicated. The player must correctly name the decimal fraction to stay on the space. If read correctly, the value in the box becomes the player's earned points. If read incorrectly, the player returns to start and his or her score returns to 0. Play continues until one player reaches the target score of 10 or more.

0.89	6.45	0.39	7.09	2.5
1.11	3.0	5.43	0.99	0.01
6.54	2.12	**Start**	0.75	1.07
1.23	1.99	0	2.33	0.3
4.44	0.07	8.11	0.79	4.08

Number and Operations: *Representing Decimals*

Patterns

 Misconception

Overgeneralization that all patterns repeat. For example, when given a sequence of numbers that requires an understanding of growth, students repeat the sequence rather than increase it (extending 1, 3, 5, 7, … as 1, 3, 5, 7, 1, 3, 5, 7, and so on rather than as 1, 3, 5, 7, 9, 11, 13, and so on, which increases by 2 each time).

What to Do

- As the study of patterns begins, make students aware that there are patterns that repeat as well as patterns that grow (see page 44).

- Use cubes, links, square tiles, and other manipulative materials to show challenging repeating patterns. Ask students to identify and extend these patterns and then create their own.

- Present students with materials they see every day and ask them to look for patterns within these things.

- Expose students to patterns that appear in nature and within their environment.

- Examine each multiplication sequence for patterns that repeat (both in the ones place and in the tens place). For example: 3, 6, 9, 12, 15, 18, 21, 24, 27, 30, 33, 36, 39, 42, 45, 48, 51, 54, 57, and so on. The "pattern unit" in the ones place is: 3, 6, 9, 2, 5, 8, 1, 4, 7, 0. The "pattern unit" in the tens place is: 0, 0, 0, 1, 1, 1, 2, 2, 2, 3, 3, 3, 3, 4, 4, 4, 5, 5, 5, 6, 6, 6, 6, and so on. Students can make predictions about what will come next in the ones and tens place and then extend this to include the hundreds place (see page 45).

- Students should use a 1–1000 chart to extend the idea of noting patterns that they've begun looking at in the early primary grades with a 1–100 chart.

- Introduce games and activities in which students need to use patterns in order to complete a task or win a game.

Look Fors

As students work through these activities, check for the following understandings:

- ✔ Students are able to describe or name the core unit or pattern core of a repeating pattern.

- ✔ Students are able to extend a repeating pattern that has a somewhat simple (AB, ABC, AAB, ABB, …) core pattern.

- ✔ Students are able to create a repeating pattern and extend it.

Name _____ Date _____

Patterns That Repeat
Patterns That Grow

Algebra—Patterns and Functions: *Patterns*

Name _____ Date _____

Patterns in Our Multiplication Facts

The ones place digit repeats at some point in every string of basic multiplication facts. Let's look at the most obvious one, the fives.

5, 10, 15, 20, 25, 30, 35, 40, ...
This is an AB (5, 0) pattern.

Write the multiples for the following factors. Circle the ones place digit and then write what the *core* unit (or what "the unit that repeats") is.

Six facts

_____, _____, _____, _____, _____, _____, _____, _____, _____, _____

Unit that repeats is: _____

Four facts

_____, _____, _____, _____, _____, _____, _____, _____, _____, _____

Unit that repeats is: _____

Eight facts

_____, _____, _____, _____, _____, _____, _____, _____, _____, _____

Unit that repeats is: _____

Three facts

_____, _____, _____, _____, _____, _____, _____, _____, _____, _____

_____, _____, _____, _____, _____, _____

Unit that repeats is: _____

Name Patterns

Write your first name over and over again (one letter per rectangle). Shade in the squares using a different color for each letter, but keep every repetition of a letter the same color.

Write about the patterns you see.

_____

_____

_____

_____

Algebra—Patterns and Functions: *Patterns*

Equals Sign and Equality

 Misconception

Interpreting the equals sign as an operator symbol. Many students interpret the equals sign to mean that an operation must be performed on the numbers to the left and that the result of this operation is recorded on the right of the equals sign. Students often ignore the equals sign when given nontraditional equations. For example, when given $4 = \underline{\hspace{1cm}} - 3$, students record "1" thinking $4 - 3 = 1$. Students also tend to view equations such as $7 = 11 - 4$, $3 + 1 = 2 + 2$, and $5 = 2 + 3$ as incorrect.

What to Do

- Provide multiple part-whole experiences to strengthen number sense. For example, students shake and spill nine bicolored counters and list all resulting combinations such as 9 and 0, 8 and 1, 7 and 2, 6 and 3, 5 and 4, and so on.

- Allow students to represent two-digit numbers in a variety of ways using connecting cubes. For example, 34 is represented as 3 sticks of ten and 4 single cubes, 2 sticks and 14 singles, 1 stick and 24 singles, and 34 single cubes.

- Provide pairs of students with a two-pan balance and weighted teddy bear counters to explore equality. These counters can be purchased from most mathematics supply catalogs. Bears come in 3 sizes (papa, mama, and baby), 3 proportional weights (12, 8, and 4 grams), and 4 colors (red, green, blue, and yellow). Encourage students to create multiple equations using the relationships among the bears. For example, 1 mama bear is equal in weight to 2 baby bears or 1M = 2B. Also, 1P = 1M + 1B or 1P = 3B.

- Provide opportunities for students to explore with a number balance. This manipulative helps students develop an understanding of equality and inequality, number comparisons, addition, and subtraction. Symbolically representing the number balance equation connects the concrete to the more abstract.

- Provide students experiences in which they create equivalent representations using Cuisenaire® Rods. For example, assign a value of 10 to the orange rod. Then ask students to find different ways to represent that value with different rods, such as 10 white rods are as long as one orange rod (see page 49).

- Let students explore unknowns in equations by placing number squares to make an equation true (see page 50).

- Ask "Is This True?" regularly and present equations that are recorded in nontraditional ways (see page 51). Expect students to support their answer with an explanation.

Look Fors

As students work through these activities, check for the following understandings:

✔ Are students able to represent numbers in different ways?

✔ Are students able to demonstrate a variety of representations of different numbers?

✔ Are students able to represent equations in various nontraditional ways?

Name _____ Date _____

Representing 10

How many different ways can the orange rod be represented? Record your work below.

The first one is done for you!

Orange rod = 10 white rods 10 = 1 + 1 + 1 + 1 + 1 + 1 + 1 + 1 + 1 + 1

Try more on the back!

Mystery Number Squares

Cut out the number squares at the bottom of the page. Place the number squares in the boxes so each equation has a balance. One number square will not be used.

$$\boxed{} = 1 + \boxed{}$$

$$6 + 8 = \boxed{} + 3$$

$$\boxed{} - 0 = \boxed{} + 1$$

Which number was not used? _____

| 10 | 11 | 12 | 13 | 14 | 15 |

Algebra—Patterns and Functions: Equals Sign and Equality

Is This True?

Is This True?   YES   NO

532 + 249 = 902 – 21

Explain why your answer makes sense.

Is This True?   YES   NO

$198 = 11 \times 18$

Explain why your answer makes sense.

Functions

 ## Misconception

Students sometimes recognize a relationship between two steps in a growing pattern and assume they have identified the functional relationship. For example, given a function table, students identify a specific relationship between two terms and apply the same rule to all terms.

What to Do

- Provide opportunities for students to explore growing patterns. Growing patterns are precursors to functional relationships (in a functional relationship, any step can be determined by the step number, without calculating all the steps in between). Students observe the step-by-step progression of a recursive pattern and continue the sequence.

- Choose or create a meaningful context for functional relationships. Examples include:

  - Money spent on candy

  - Ingredients needed for a recipe

  - Time required to finish a race

  - Fuel needed for a vacation

- Allow students to construct physical models of functional relationships using tiles, toothpicks, connecting cubes, or other hands-on materials. The act of placing toothpicks in a specified pattern or connecting cubes in a sequence can provide insight into the relationship between the two variables.

- Compare physical models with pictorial or symbolic representations. For example, consider the growing pattern of triangles in "Making Triangles," page 54.

- Model the language of the dependent relationship and encourage students to describe the relationship. Examples include:

  - *The amount of money I spend depends on how much candy I buy.*

  - *The number of cups of flour needed is determined by the number of pancakes we would like to make.*

  - *The time required to complete the race is a function of the distance of the race.*

  - *The amount of fuel we use is directly related to the miles traveled.*

- Reinforce number sense through estimation. When students are able to articulate their intuitive understanding of the relationship, they may estimate and solve the function simultaneously.

- Have students graph the relationships revealed in a function as a visual picture while learning about rates of change (see page 55).

Look Fors

As students work through these activities, check for the following understandings:

✔ Students test their rule for the pattern among many terms to confirm the rule is correct.

✔ Students are able to describe a rule verbally as well as pictorially.

✔ Students can extend increasing and decreasing patterns.

Name _____ Date _____

Building Toothpick Bridges

Look at the pattern of bridges below. How many toothpicks would be needed to build a bridge with 10 spans? Complete the table and explain how you got your answer

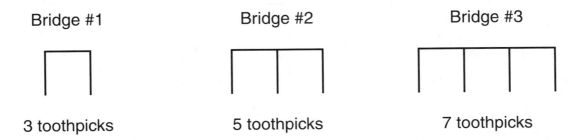

Bridge #1   Bridge #2   Bridge #3

3 toothpicks   5 toothpicks   7 toothpicks

Number of Toothpicks Needed to Build Bridges

Bridge Spans	1	2	3	4	5	6	7	8	9	10
Number of Toothpicks Needed	3	5	7							

I know my answer is correct because . . .

Name _____ Date _____

Making Triangles

Step #	Step 1	Step 2	Step 3	Step 4	Step 5
Representation	△	▱	◺◹	◺◹◺	◺◹◺◹
Perimeter	3 units	4 units	5 units	6 units	7 units

1.   What rule could be used to explain the functional relationship between the number of triangles and the perimeter of the figure?

2.   What would be the perimeter of the figure that included 100 triangles? How do you know?

3.   How would the rule change if the pattern were made with squares rather than triangles? Use words and or pictures to explain your answer.

Algebra—Patterns and Functions: *Functions*

Name _____ Date _____

Cheaper by the Dozen

The Student Council is planning to raise money for field trips by selling water bottles in the school store. The more water bottles purchased, the cheaper the price.

Catalog Prices for Water Bottles

Cases of bottles	1	2	3	4	5	6	7
Price	$20	$38	$54	$68	$80	$90	$98

Sketch a graph in the space below to show the relationship between the price and the number of cases purchased. Let the *x*-axis represent the number of cases and the *y*-axis show the price.

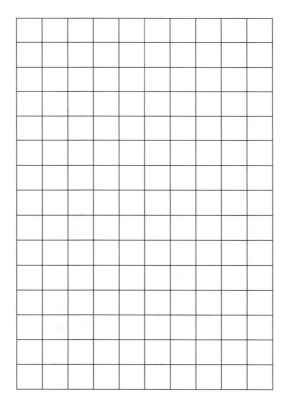

Variables

 ## Misconception

A lack of understanding about place value and computation yields an inability to use a variable as a digit in an equation.

What to Do

- Have students identify the elements in a repeating pattern with letters of the alphabet. Students will probably already know how to do this (from earlier grades), but reinforce that a circle, square, triangle core unit may also be called an ABC pattern.

- Label polygons with letters identifying each vertex of the shape (see page 58). Middle school students aren't confused when they see this and neither should third- through fifth-grade students. When learning about angles in geometry class it seems perfectly sensible to have fifth graders identify these angles with letters that correspond.

- Have students look for places where a letter is used to represent some word. "Mathematical Equations" can be created where students replace the letter with the word that makes the equation "true." (See page 60.) **Following is the answer key:** Answers: 10 = digits in our numeration system; 12 = numerals on an analog clock; 4 = seasons in a year; 31 = days in January, March, May, July, August, October, and December; 60 = minutes in an hour, 60 = seconds in a minute; 24 = hours in a day; 100 = years in a century

- Point out how letters are used in formulas that are being learned. Before students learn formulas to determine the area and perimeter of polygons or the volume of solid figures, they should know the words that the letters represent.

- Begin replacing the "box" in an arithmetic equation with a letter.

$$n + 13 = 27 \qquad 34 - n = 12 \qquad 61 = n - 27$$

Look Fors

As students work through these activities, check for the following understandings:

- ✔ Students aren't just looking at the digits and the sign and then following the sign. Be sure they are trying to make sense of the open expression.

- ✔ Students are using a letter to label things that might have been assigned a numeral (length of a rectangle).

- ✔ Students can use a number balance to determine the missing addend or sum.

Name _____ Date _____

Algebra Challenge

Use the digits 0, 1, 2, 3, 4, 5, 6, 7, 8, and 9 to make the equation below true. If you have the same letter, you need to use the same digit. (For example, If "A" = 3, all As must equal a 3.)

This challenge has many correct answers. Try to get at least one.

$$\begin{array}{r} \text{M A N} \\ + \text{F A N} \\ \hline \text{M E L T} \end{array}$$

Using Letters as Labels

Look at the different polygons below and use letters to identify specific information about these shapes.

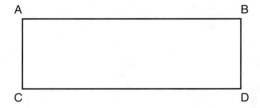

Use letters to name this *rectangle*. _____
Use letters to name one *right angle*. _____

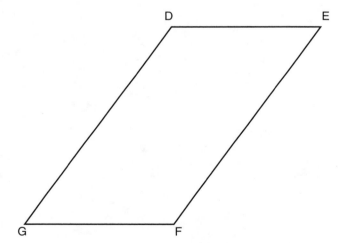

Use letters to name this *parallelogram*. _____
Use letters to name one *acute angle*. _____
Use letters to name one *obtuse angle*. _____

Algebra—Patterns and Functions: *Variables*

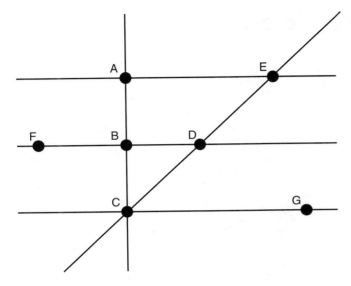

Use letters to name one triangle.

Use letters to name one trapezoid.

Use letters to name one right angle.

Use letters to name one acute angle.

Name _____ Date _____

Mathematical Equations

1. 10 = D. in our N. S.

2. 12 = N. on an A. C.

3. 4 = S. in a Y.

4. 31 = D. in J., M., M., J., A., O., and D.

5. 60 = M. in an H.

6. 60 = S. in a M.

7. 24 = H. in a D.

8. 100 = Y. in a C.

Algebra—Patterns and Functions: *Variables*

Algebraic Representation

 Misconception

Teachers sometimes use representations to show students how to understand a mathematics concept, rather than using representations to show how a student is thinking about a mathematical situation. For example, teachers may incorrectly assume that when students use manipulatives, doing so "teaches" them the concept. It is critical to ask students to explain their representation.

What to Do

- Provide opportunities for students to explore, and then talk about, a variety of manipulatives. Model the correct vocabulary that is specific to each manipulative. Plan lessons in which students use these manipulatives.

- Encourage students' use of multiple representations. Create and model an environment in which all explanations and representations are honored.

- Allow students to freely select from different representations to use in solving any problem. Initially, model conventional ways of representing mathematical situations, but eventually allow students opportunities to choose representations that they are comfortable using. Knowing which type of representation is useful in which situation is an important milestone in mathematical understanding and reasoning for students.

- Ask students to explain and show how they are thinking about a problem during and following a problem-solving task. When students hear how others use representations to show how they are thinking about a mathematical idea, it helps them to consider other perspectives. Communicating their thinking requires students to reflect on their problem solving and reasoning; listening to students' explanations enables teachers to determine what students know and can do at any point in time.

- Provide opportunities for students to solve many open-ended tasks with a representation they have chosen. Follow these problem-solving tasks with classroom discussions.

- Model for students how to record their way of solving a problem using numbers. Be sure to record the students' methods both horizontally and vertically.

- Observe when students use a representation to determine if they understand the representation and how to use it to effectively solve the problem.

- Use literature to engage students in problem solving and ask them to represent their solutions in a representation that makes sense to them (see page 62).

Look Fors

As students work through these activities, check for the following understandings:

- ✔ Students' flexibility in their use of representations to show their thinking.

- ✔ Student use of appropriate vocabulary in describing a strategy or representation.

Algebraic Representation

Algebra Bibliography

Andreasen, Dan. 2007. *The Baker's Dozen: A Counting Book*. New York: Henry Holt.

This story describes the sweets a baker prepares before his shop opens. He begins with one éclair, two cakes, and all the way up to twelve cupcakes. Once the story has been read, ask students to figure out how many total sweets have been baked and to show how they know in a representation. Ask students to show their answer in a different representation. Challenge them to choose the most efficient way of solving the problem and explain why this is so.

Giganti, Paul Jr. 1988. *How Many Snails? A Counting Book*. New York: Greenwillow Books.

A delightful book that asks a series of questions for students to use visual analysis to determine and count the number of objects on illustrated pages, which are similar yet different. Ask students to use symbolic representations when they share counting results. This experience helps students develop their understanding of representations using arithmetic expressions. Once students are familiar with the language pattern in the book, provide time for them to represent additional "pages." Combine these into a class book.

Merriam, Eve. 1993. *12 Ways to Get to 11*. New York: Aladdin Paperbacks.

In this engaging book, twelve different ways to get to eleven are demonstrated on illustrated pages. Ask students to represent the different ways (for example, three turtles, two frogs, one lily pond, and five dragonflies). The different ways support children in symbolic representation. Challenge children to find all the different ways to get to a different number. Adjust the target number so that it is appropriate for the grade you are teaching.

Nagda, Ann Whitehead, and Cindy Bickel. 2000. *Tiger Math*. New York: Henry Holt.

The growth of a Siberian tiger cub is chronicled with a series of different types of graphs that demonstrate the progress of his growth. These graph representations can serve as a springboard for interpreting mathematical relationships in many forms.

Name _____ Date _____

Favorite Fruits

Take a poll of your classmates to find out which fruit is preferred: lemon, strawberry, or apple. Show your results below in a graph.

What do you notice about the information in your graph? Show this information using both words and numbers.

Algebra—Patterns and Functions: *Algebraic Representation*

Fruit Logic Problem

Fourth Graders' Favorite Fruit						
Lemon	🍋	▲				
Raspberry	🫐	▲	▲			
Apple	🍎	▲	▲	▲	▲	▲
Banana	🍌	▲	▲	▲	▲	

▲ = 5 students

Use the clues to determine each student's favorite snack from the information the fourth graders collected about their favorite fruit:

Nick likes the fruit whose total is an odd number.

Heather likes the fruit that is double the amount of the least chosen fruit.

Theresa likes the fruit whose total is a prime number.

Eli likes the fruit that is a multiple of 2, 4, 5, and 10.

Nick: _____   Theresa: _____

Heather: _____   Eli: _____

Algebra—Patterns and Functions: *Algebraic Representation*

Explain how you know your answers are correct.

Two-Dimensional Figures

 Misconception

Categorizing two-dimensional shapes incorrectly due to overgeneralizing from incorrect examples or the orientation of the shape.

What to Do

- Go on a shape hunt and have students identify shapes in their classroom, school, and home environment.

- Combine geometry with number concepts by having students find different shapes on an activity pages.

- Select math-related literature that shows children accurate plane figures.

- Develop "concept cards" of examples and nonexamples (see page 68).

- Develop some "best examples" ("clear cases demonstrating the variation of the concept's attributes" [Tennyson, Youngers, and Suebsonthi 1983, 281*]) for each of the two- and three-dimensional shapes included in your curriculum. Ask students questions about these examples to determine whether they recognize the important properties of each.

- Encourage students to describe, draw, model, identify, and classify shapes, as well as predict what the results would be for combining and decomposing these.

- Take care in selecting posters, math-related literature, and other commercial displays. Often these tools include inaccurate examples of shapes (show rectangles with only two long and two short sides)

or incorrect shapes (ellipses that are labeled "ovals" and rhombi that are labeled "diamonds").

- Allow students to create shapes from a variety of materials so they see regular as well as irregular shapes.

- Have students use Venn diagrams to list common attributes of figures and to classify figures. This activity will extend their definitions and provide them with visual representations of various shapes.

- Play games like "Guess My Shape," where clues are given, students draw a shape after each clue, and then determine the shape being described after all the clues have been read.

- Incorporate other areas of geometry into activities with shapes (such as creating tessellations and transforming shapes through rotations, translations, and reflections, as well as combining shapes) to give students opportunities to spend more time manipulating and exploring with plane figures.

Look Fors

- ✔ Listen to hear if students are able to classify shapes in a variety of ways.

- ✔ Look to see if students can name shapes regardless of their position.

- ✔ Watch to see if students are able to create both regular and irregular polygons.

*Tennyson, R. D., J. Youngers, and P. Suebsonthi. 1983. "Concept Learning of Children Using Instructional Presenting Forms for Prototype Formation and Classification-Skill Development." *Journal of Education Psychology* 75:280–91.

Categorizing Quadrilaterals

Look at the 10 quadrilaterals below and think about what you know about each shape. Then use the chart to identify all of the squares, rectangles, parallelograms, rhombuses, and trapezoids. Write the letter from the shape in the column of the chart.

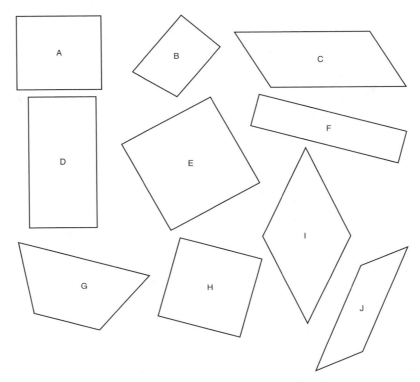

*Remember that some shapes might belong to more than one category.

Squares	Rectangles	Parallelograms	Rhombi	Trapezoids

Name _____ Date _____

Sorting Two-Dimensional Shapes

Cut out these shapes and decide on different ways to sort them. Then explain, in writing, how you sorted the shapes and make observations about the groups that were made.

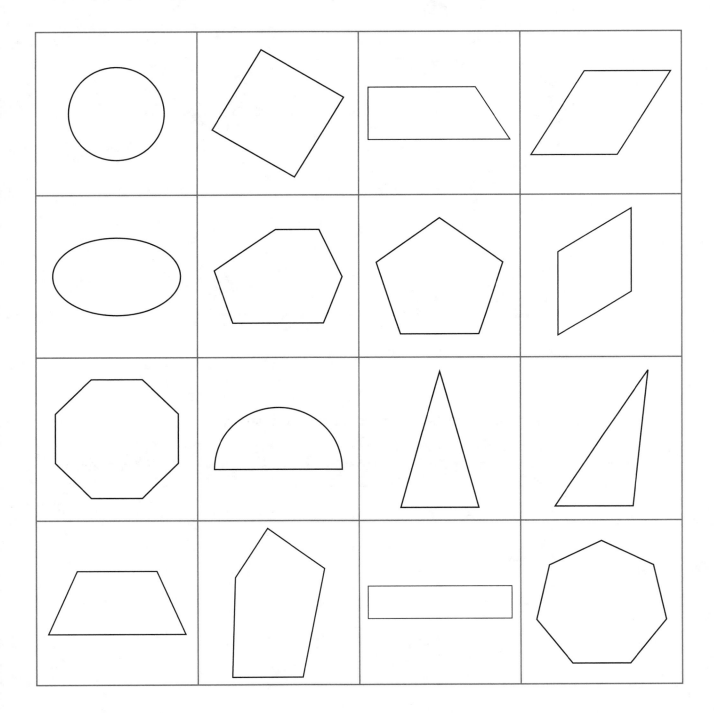

Name _____ Date _____

Logical Reasoning with Nonsense Figures

Use the figures below to figure out what a *flix* is.

All of these are flix:

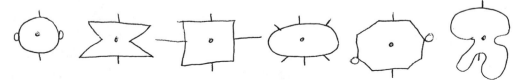

None of these is a flix:

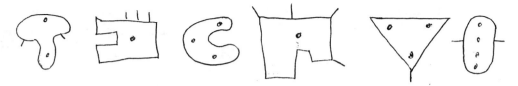

Which of these are flix?

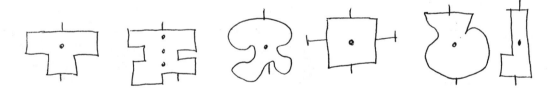

Use the figures below to figure out what a *nint* is.

All of these are nints:

R 2 d m 5 p n

None of these is a nint:

S L 7 M 8 6 N v

Which of these are nints?

Three-Dimensional Figures

 Misconception

Calling a three-dimensional figure by the name of one of its faces. For example, students may call a cube a square.

What to Do

- Look at various objects in the classroom (the door, cabinet shelves, the globe, dice) and name these figures correctly. These geometry words should be placed on a mathematics word wall, along with various pictures or other real objects and wooden or foam objects that are made from these solid figures.

- Offer a range of activities in which students find, color, name, and discuss the solid figures they need to learn and ask open-ended questions to ensure that the attributes of these figures are clarified. For example: "Is it OK for this to be a cone even though it's smaller than this cone?" "Can this still be a cylinder even though it's turned this way?" "Would this still be called a sphere if it were made out of plastic?"

- Ask students to determine the number of vertices, faces, and edges each figure has, and be sure to have them name the plane figures making up these faces/surfaces. Unfolding and then refolding "nets," made of cardstock, allows students to decompose these figures to better see what each is made out of.

- Play "Guess the Shape" (see page 71), which provides students with a logical thinking activity while it reinforces the name of the solid figure and the plane figures as well as other characteristics. **Answers to "Guess the Shape"**: cube, cone, cylinder.

- Provide students with geometric analogies so that they begin to look at the attributes of specific solid figures and see the difference between these and plane figures (see page 72).

- Teach students how to draw various three-dimensional figures. Students love creating objects from these figures once they have learned how to draw them. Be sure to discuss the attributes of these figures, naming the surfaces as plane figures.

- Have students listen to *The Important Book*, by Margaret Wise Brown. Give every four students a different labeled picture of a solid figure. Use a sphere, cube, cone, cylinder, pyramid, and rectangular prism. Have students first brainstorm things that the shape reminds them of and then attributes of the figure. Reread *The Important Book* and ask students what style the author is using on each page. Have them then work together to create their own page in a book, which will be called *The Important Thing About Solid Figures*.

Look Fors

As students work through these activities, check for the following understandings:

- ✔ Are students able to describe and classify geometric solids in a variety of ways?

- ✔ Can students name geometric solids regardless of their position?

Guess the Shape

- ■ This solid figure has 6 surfaces/faces.

- ■ This solid figure is made of rectangles.

- ■ This solid figure has 8 vertices.

- ■ The faces of this solid figure make right angles with the bases.

- ■ All of the faces are squares.

What shape is this?

- ■ This solid figure has a circular base.

- ■ This solid figure has an axis that is perpendicular to its base.

- ■ This solid figure has a surface from the boundary of the base to its vertex.

What shape is this?

- ■ This solid figure has 2 congruent parallel bases.

- ■ The bases of this solid figure may or may not be circular.

- ■ When opened the surface of this solid figure is a rectangle.

What shape is this?

Geometric Analogies

Use the examples to the left to help you complete the example to the right. Select the correct answer from the selection given to you.

Geometry: *Three-Dimensional Figures*

The Important Thing About . . .

Read *The Important Book*, by Margaret Wise Brown. Give pairs of students a solid figure and have them generate writing, in the same style as the author, for their shape. Have them draw things that are shaped like this figure after their writing is completed.

The important thing about a _____ is that it's_____

_____

_____

_____

_____

_____

_____

_____

Coordinate Geometry

Misconception

Incorrectly naming points or spaces on a coordinate grid.

What to Do

- Encourage students to articulate descriptions of location, direction, and distance related to current or future positions. Generate a list of vocabulary words for each of the three categories, such as:

  - Location: *over, under, behind, between, above, below*

  - Direction: *left, right, up, down, north, south, east, west, clockwise*

  - Distance: *near, far, long, short, inches, miles*

  Create a series of steps using these words, and allow students to act them out in order to reach a specific destination. When students generate directions for others to follow, or attempt the follow the directions of their peers, they become aware of the importance of direction and distance when seeking location.

- With a small group, construct a grid with a large piece of graph paper. Let each student choose a unique game piece and place it on the grid. Students should name the location and then respond to such questions as:

  - How would you describe your location compared to mine?

  - How far are you from the origin?

  - Which is the shortest path for you to reach another student?

  - Do you share a coordinate with anyone else?

- Provide activities for students to plot points and additional activities that require students to name spaces. The game "Where's Blazer" requires students to plot points (see page 77). However, when playing such commercial games as Connect Four™ and Battleship™, students name spaces. It is important for students to have experiences with both and to distinguish between the two.

- Make connections to real-world applications using stories and maps.

  - Include students in the planning of an upcoming field trip. Use maps to find the destination, plan the direction needed to travel, determine the distance using the scale, and calculate the approximate time of arrival.

  - Allow students to plan a scavenger hunt. Let them draw maps and provide clues for each stop along the path to the final treasure (see page 76).

  - Use a city street map (grid) to explore the notion of multiple ways to get from one place to another, all being the same distance but traveling in different directions.

- Expand the coordinate grid to include negative values when students are ready (perhaps just two quadrants and then four). This activity provides a larger medium for the application of symmetry, congruence, and transformations.

Look Fors

As students work through these activities, check for the following understandings:

✔ Are students able to correctly identify the coordinates for a specific space/point?

✔ Can students navigate the coordinate grid by describing location, distance, and direction?

Scavenger Hunt

Fold an 18″ × 24″ piece of white paper to form 16 congruent rectangles. Lightly trace the folds to make a grid, as shown below.

Draw a treasure map over the grid using crayons or color pencils.

On a separate sheet of paper, write specific directions to identify the location of the treasure.

Trade maps with a partner and follow one another's directions to find the treasure. Offer advice if the directions need additional descriptors of location, direction, or distance.

Name _____ Date _____

Where's Blazer?

Cut out the picture of Blazer below and place him at any point on the grid. Name his location. Describe the moves needed to get Blazer back home, naming each point along the way.

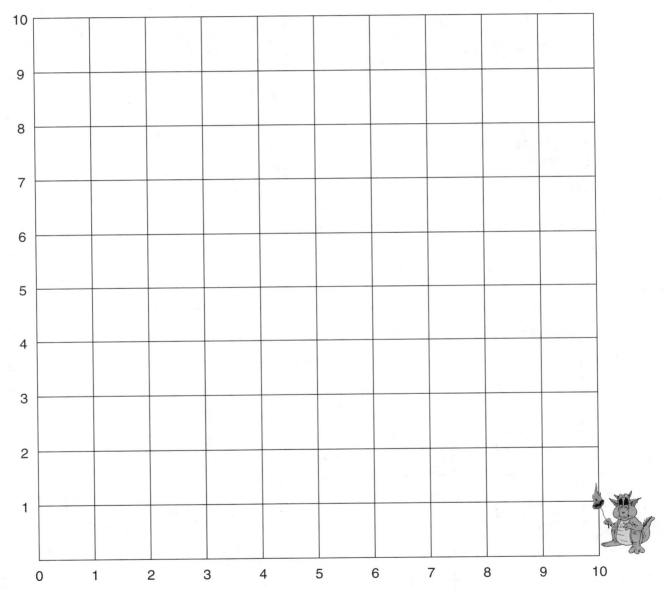

Project the game board and play as a class, or allow students to play in small groups to guess the predetermined hiding place for Blazer. Allow students to name points, and provide directional clues based on each guess.

....

Geometry: *Coordinate Geometry*

Four in a Row

Each player uses a different color crayon. Take turns naming the coordinates of a space. If the other players agree the space is named correctly, the player may color the space. The object of the game is to be the first to color in four spaces in a row, either vertically, horizontally, or diagonally.

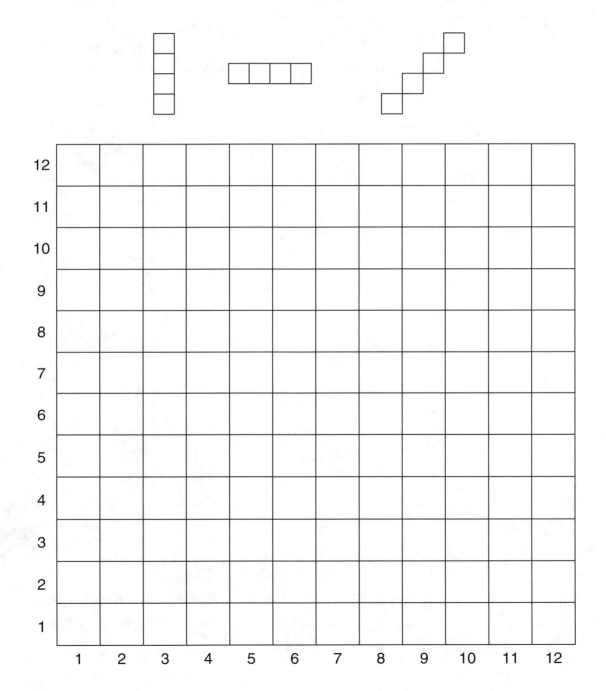

Geometry: *Coordinate Geometry*

Transformations, Symmetry, and Congruence

Misconception

Overgeneralizing the line of reflection due to limited concrete experiences with transformations. For example, students identify the reflection line, rather than the movement of the figures, as the type of reflection occurring.

What to Do

- Allow students to role-play flips (reflections), slides (translations), and turns (rotations) with their bodies. For example, ask students to sit on the floor with legs crossed and *slide* backward.

- Provide students experiences with pattern blocks, attribute blocks, or tangram puzzles. They naturally use transformations when creating designs or pictures. Ask them to explain how a design or picture was made to reinforce transformational vocabulary.

- Find all possible arrangements for five squares (see pages 80–81).

- Let students use materials to model vertical, horizontal, and diagonal reflections across a line of reflection. Place tangram puzzles in a center area. Copy the Line of Reflection template (page 82) for students to investigate *vertical reflections* over a horizontal axis of reflection or *horizontal reflections* across a vertical axis of reflection.

- Make rotation tools (see page 83). Students rotate a figure around *a point* to view how its position looks at different points (for example, quarter- or half-turns).

- Allow students to investigate transformations on the computer. The National Council of Teachers of Mathematics has links to a variety of programs on the Illuminations website. Kid Pix or Geometer's Sketchpad are options as well.

- Show examples and nonexamples of symmetrical designs and pictures.

- Model how to place a mirror perpendicular to a design or picture to show a symmetrical reflection. Place several mirrors in a center area with a variety of pictures so students can further explore symmetry.

- Provide paper-folding experiences. For example, students fold a paper in half, cut out a design on the fold, and then open the paper to reveal a symmetrical design.

- Provide geoboards for students to create symmetrical designs or pictures. Geoboards allow concrete experience with rotational symmetry. Students make a design on geoboard and predict how it will look when turned or rotated. They record predictions on dot geoboard paper and check their predictions by actually turning the geoboard.

Look Fors

As students work through these activities, check for the following understandings:

✔ Are students able to describe and model transformations accurately?

✔ Are students able to recognize, model, and describe symmetry and congruence?

Five Squares: How Many Arrangements Are Possible?

For this investigation, students will find all possible arrangments for 5 squares. Students use visualization and spatial reasoning skills when they apply transformations: slides (translations), flips (reflections), and turns (rotations).

You will need the following materials:

- 1″ color tiles, 1 bucket per 4 students

- 1″ square grid paper, 2 or 3 per student

- scissors, 1 per student

- crayons or markers

Explain that there are rules to follow when making their arrangements:

- Each square tile must have at least 1 whole side touching another.

   This is OK. **This is not OK.**

- Each arrangement must be different.

- Sliding, flipping, and turning are required when checking whether a new arrangement is different.

Ask a volunteer to arrange 2 color tiles on an overhead projector. This figure, called a *domino*, has only 1 possible arrangement. If students say there are 2 different arrangements, show how to rotate arrangement to show they are the same. Repeat with 3 color tiles (which is called a *triomino* and has 2 possible arrangements). Finally, students arrange 4 color tiles (called a *tetromino* and having 5 possible arrangements).

Ask students to find all the different possible arrangements for 5 squares, a *pentomino*.

Distribute color tiles, grid paper, and markers. Students use color tiles to explore arrangements. Arrangements are recorded on grid paper. They cut out their arrangements and slide, flip, or turn them to check whether any arrangement has already been made.

For students who complete the task before the others, challenge them to think about which arrangements could be folded into a box without a lid (without actually folding).

Allow students to explain their strategies in determining that all possible different arrangements were found. Some students may notice that arrangements resemble letters of the alphabet and can use this as a way to check arrangements. It is recommended that you not tell students there are 12 arrangements possible. This helps support a richer investigation of the task!

Note: A more detailed lesson with a student dialogue is described in *Introduction to Reasoning and Proof, Grades 3–5* by K. Schultz-Ferrell, B. Hammond, and J. Robles (The Math Process Standard Series, S. O'Connell, Series Ed. Portsmouth, NH: Heinemann, 2007).

Line of Reflection Template

Geometry: *Transformations, Symmetry, and Congruence*

Name _____ Date _____

Rotation Tools

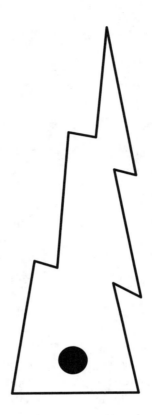

Cut out the shape below. Fasten it to the above shape using a brad or paper fastener.

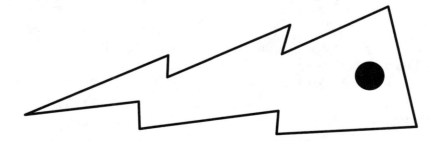

Spatial Problem Solving

Misconception

Inability to create mental images of objects.

What to Do

- Provide visualization opportunities for students to develop their "mind's eye" (see page 86).

- Allow students to manipulate and build structures using a variety of materials, such as multilink cubes, wooden blocks, and connecting cubes. These tactile experiences provide students with opportunities to view different transformations of figures.

- Present small groups of students with several nets and geometric solids. Challenge the students to match each net to the solid they predict the net would form when cut and folded. Allow students to confirm their predictions by cutting and folding the nets to form solids. Students may also trace the faces of a solid to form their own net.

- Let students make two-dimensional representations of three-dimensional figures using Cartesian graph paper or isometric graph paper (available free online). See page 87.

- Ask students to draw various polygons using a ruler. Students may then cut out the polygons and slice each by drawing a line segment connecting any two points on the polygon. Encourage students to name the original polygon and the two new polygons created. Challenge students to:

  - Slice a triangle to make a trapezoid and a triangle

  - Slice a pentagon to make two quadrilaterals

  - Slice a hexagon to make two pentagons

- Allow students to fold a sheet of paper in half and make a single cut through the two layers (like making a heart shape or a snowflake). Ask students to describe to a partner what the image will look like before unfolding. Students may then unfold the sheet and discuss how their prediction compared to the final image.

- Provide students with pictures and/or photographs of structures such as buildings, bridges, and playground equipment. Ask students to identify geometric shapes and solids, examples of symmetry, and transformations they see within the pictures. Invite students to continue the search for additional pictures by browsing magazines.

- Provide puzzles for students to complete. Many are commercially available using such math resources as:

  - Rectangles using a complete set of pentominoes

  - Symmetry and reflection using GeoReflectors™

- Expose students to real-world applications of two-dimensional drawings such as blueprints, house plans, or aerial-view photographs.

■ Present students with sets of cards showing the top, front, and side view of figures made with connecting cubes. Students can then construct the figures using the visual clues. Let students make their own figures and create the corresponding clue cards of each view (see page 88).

■ Look for geometric shapes and figures in works of art. Some suggestions include: *Three Musicians* (Pablo Picasso); *Cubi Series* (David Smith); *Broken Obelisk* (Barnett Newman)*; Hand with Reflecting Sphere* (M. C. Escher).

Look Fors

As students work through these activities, check for the following understandings:

✔ Can students describe shapes and figures and relate them to real-world objects?

✔ Are students able to match two-dimensional representations with the corresponding three-dimensional objects?

✔ Are students able to describe mental images of objects?

Name _____ Date _____

Draw What You Saw

Choose one of the images below and transfer it to a projector. Flash the image for students to see for just a few seconds. Instruct students to draw what they saw. Finally, show image again so students can compare their representations to the original. Repeat the process with another image.

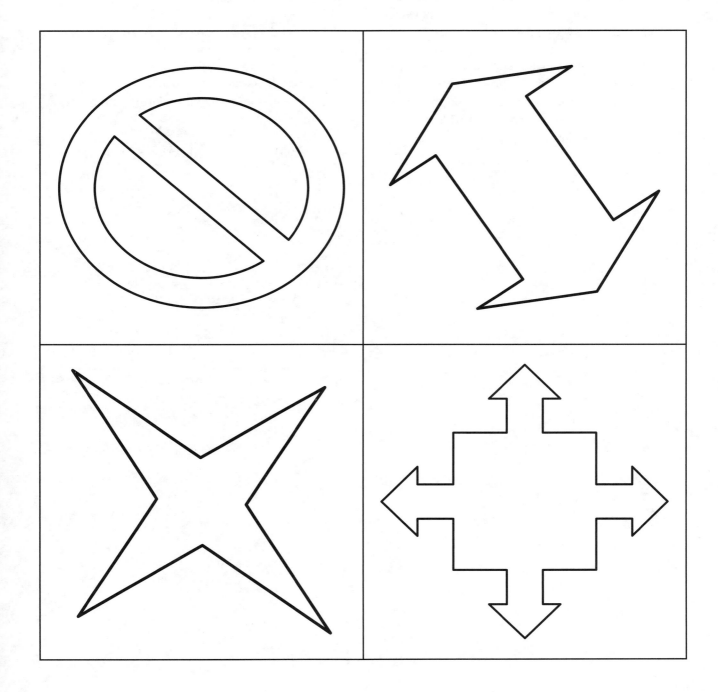

Geometry: *Spatial Problem Solving*

From 3-D to 2-D

Choose a geometric solid to draw on the grid paper below. An example of a rectangular prism has been provided.

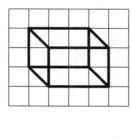
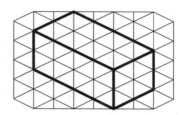

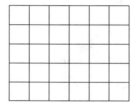
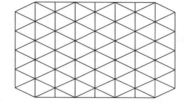

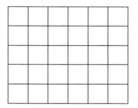
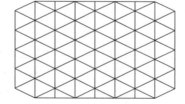

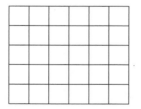
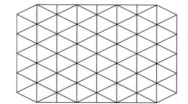

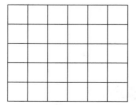
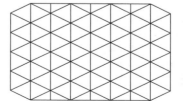

View and Build

Use blocks or connecting cubes to build the figures below.

Figure #1 Front View	Figure #1 Top View	Figure #1 Side View
Figure #2 Front View	**Figure #2** Top View	**Figure #2** Side View
Figure #3 Front View	**Figure #3** Top View	**Figure #3** Side View
Make Your Own Front View	Make Your Own Top View	Make Your Own Side View

Geometry: *Spatial Problem Solving*

Telling Time on an Analog Clock

 Misconception

The hour hand and minute hand are confused, or the student names the numeral closest to the hour hand regardless of whether this is appropriate. For example, when given the time of 2:45 on an analog clock, students say that it's 2:09, 9:02, forty-five minutes past three, ten minutes past nine.

What to Do

- Using an hour-hand-only clock position the hand directly on a numeral and have students say the o'clock time. Then position the hand halfway between two numerals and have students say the half-hour time. Do the same for the quarter past, quarter of, and three-quarters past times.

- Have students match clock faces with phrase cards to connect the time vocabulary with the face on an analog clock (see page 90).

- Play "How Many Minutes After?" which has students making a connection between the numeral that the minute hand is pointing to and the number of minutes after the hour this represents (see page 92).

- Provide students with story problems that give them practice drawing the hands on an analog clock face, writing the digital time, and working on elapsed-time problems where they write to explain how they got their answer (see pages 92 and 93).

Look Fors

As students work through these activities, check for the following understandings:

- ✔ Can students correctly match the phrase, digital time, and analog clock face?

- ✔ Do students have a strategy for determining the number of minutes after the hour each of the numerals on a clock face represents?

- ✔ Are students able to articulate different ways to say the time at quarter-hour intervals?

- ✔ Can students solve elapsed-time problems and write to explain how their answer was obtained?

Name _____   Date _____

Matching Time (Clocks) and
Time (Phrases) and Time (Digital)

Cut out the twelve "clock" cards. Then cut out the twelve "time word" cards. Match the sets of cards until all of the cards have been used up.

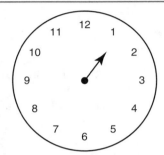
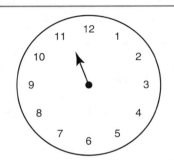

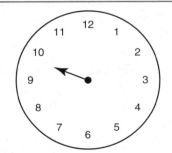
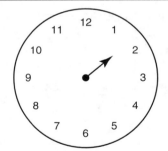

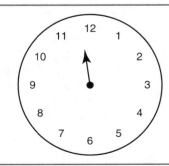
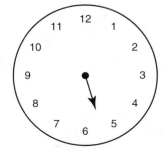
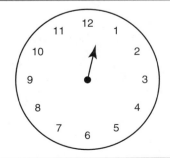

Measurement: *Telling Time on an Analog Clock*

5:30	4:15	1:45
3:30	11:15	12:30
6:45	1:15	5:45
8:15	9:45	11:45

half past three	a quarter to six	a quarter of two
a quarter after eight	half past twelve	a quarter to seven
a quarter after eleven	a quarter to twelve	a quarter after four
half past five	a quarter of ten	a quarter after one

How Many Minutes After?

Toss 2 numeral cubes. Use what you see to fill in the chart below. Do this 7 times to practice connecting the numerals on the clock to the number of minutes after the hour.

I tossed:	This total is:	Draw the minute hand on the clock	Minutes after the hour?
▢ ▢	_____	(clock)	_____
▢ ▢	_____	(clock)	_____
▢ ▢	_____	(clock)	_____
▢ ▢	_____	(clock)	_____
▢ ▢	_____	(clock)	_____
▢ ▢	_____	(clock)	_____
▢ ▢	_____	(clock)	_____

Measurement: *Telling Time on an Analog Clock*

Name _____ Date _____

Story Problems for Elapsed Time

For each problem, use whatever strategy works to help you get your answer. Draw the hour and minute hands on the clock to show your answer and write the digital time that shows your answer. Don't forget to explain what you did to get your answer.

Michael wakes up at 6:30 a.m. It takes him 15 minutes to wash up, 10 minutes to get dressed, 5 minutes to make his bed, and 15 minutes to eat his breakfast. Then he leaves for school. What time is it when Michael leaves for school?

Draw an analog clock   Draw a digital clock face

_____

_____

Warren walks to school. He leaves his house at 7:20. It takes him 25 minutes to get to school. What time does he arrive?

Draw an analog clock   Draw a digital clock face

_____

_____

Measurement: *Telling Time on an Analog Clock*

Determining the Value of Coins

 ## Misconception

Organizing coins first is not necessary for efficient counting of money. When counting coins in an unorganized manner, students count on from different coins and use inconsistent skip-counting sequences.

What to Do

- Use children's literature to pose problem-solving questions that support students' understanding of counting larger amounts (see page 95).

- Skip-count by 5s, 10s, 25s, and 50s. Use coins to help facilitate skip counting.

- Play "Earn $1.00." Each pair of students will need real coins (pennies, nickels, dimes, and quarters), a $1.00 bill, 2 dice, and 2 work mats. Partners take turn rolling the dice and adding the total showing on dice. They place that many pennies on their work mat. A partner may exchange any coins collected on a turn when appropriate as long as the amount remains the same.

- Give a signal when a shift occurs in counting money by one number. Use only two types of coins initially. For example, using 3 dimes and 2 nickels, point to the dimes and ask students to count (10¢, 20¢, 30¢). Hold up your hand to indicate a pause, and then bring your hand down. Point to the nickels and continue to count (35¢, 40¢). Add additional types of coins, each time pausing between counts that require a different type of counting. See *Teaching Student-Centered Mathematics* (Van de Walle and Lovin 2006, 151*) for more detail.

- Provide opportunities for students to place coin amounts in order according to their values. First, check students' abilities to put numerals in order beginning with greatest number. For example, 1, 10, 1, 5, 25, 10, 1, and 5. Students line up as 25,

10, 10, 5, 5, 1, 1, 1. This helps them organize coin sets before determining their value.

- Provide 100-charts for students to visually and concretely see the amount of pennies in nickels, dimes, and quarter (Drum and Petty 1999, 264–68*).

- Encourage students to mentally add numbers that represent the values of different coins. For example, record 10, 25, 5, 5, 1, 1, and 50 on the board in a random arrangement and ask students to add them mentally.

- Target an amount and challenge students to find all the possible ways to make that amount using pennies, nickels, dimes, quarters, or half-dollars. Ask them to explain how they know they have found all the ways possible.

- Provide opportunities for students to solve logic riddles about coins. Expect students to justify possible answers after each line of a riddle is read (see page 96).

Look Fors

As students work through these activities, check for the following understandings:

✔ Are students able to organize coin sets before determining the value?

✔ Can students find multiple ways to make a given amount?

Determining the Value of Coins

Money Bibliography

Allen, Nancy K. 1999. *Once Upon a Dime, A Math Adventure*. Watertown, MA: Charlesbridge.

> Farmer Worth grows a money tree and leaves for China with his bumper crop. He leaves the running of the farm to a boy. Students total the amount of money the boy "grows."

Axelrod, Amy. 1997. *Pigs Will Be Pigs: Fun with Math and Money*. New York: Aladdin.

> The Pig family searches their house for spare change in order to pay for dinner. Students total all the money found.

Burns, Marilyn. 1990. *The $1.00 Word Riddle Book*. White Plains, NY: Math Solutions.

> The riddles in this book give students clues for finding words worth $1.00 ($a$ = $.01, b = $.02, c = $.03, and so on). One hundred $1.00 words are explored.

Maestro, Betsy. 1993. *The Story of Money*. New York: Clarion Books.

> This book begins in prehistoric times and traces the use of money through five thousand years of recorded history to modern times.

Rocklin, Joanne. 1998. *The Case of the $hrunken Allowance*. New York: Scholastic.

> Friends investigate P. B.'s claim that his allowance has shrunk. Engage students in exploring different combinations for $10.05, which was how much P. B. saved.

Williams, Rozanne L. 2001. *The Coin Counting Book*. Watertown, MA: Charlesbridge.

> This book contains coin-counting opportunities with photographs of real coins.

Zimelman, Nathan. 2000. *Sold! A Mathematics Adventure*. Watertown, MA: Charlesbridge.

> A boy purchases too many "useless" things at an auction, but one item is worth a fortune. Ask students to explore other items they think are worth $28,000,000.

*Van de Wall, J. and L. Lovin. 2006. *Teaching Student–Centered Mathematics: K–3*. Boston: Pearson Ed.

*Drum, R. and W. Petty, Jr. 1999. "Teaching the Value of Coins." *Teaching Children Mathematics*. Reston, VA: NCTM.

Determining the Value of Coins

Prepare 4 envelopes with the following amounts: $1.42 (5 quarters, 3 nickels, 2 pennies), $.35 (7 nickels), $.45 (1 quarter, 4 nickels), and $.90 (2 quarters, 4 dimes).

Reveal one line in a riddle at a time. Expect students to justify possible answers after each line is revealed.

Coin Riddle #1

There are 10 coins in the envelope.
Half of them are the same coin with a coin value that is a double-digit number.
This double-digit value is a square number.
There is one more nickel than pennies.
What is the amount in the envelope?

Coin Riddle #2

There are 7 coins in the envelope.
The value of each coin is an odd number.
The value of each coin is a prime number.
The value of all the coins is 35¢.
What coins are in the envelope?

Coin Riddle #3

There are 5 coins in the envelope.
The total value of the coins in the envelope is a multiple of 3.
The total value is less than $.48.
There is 1 quarter.
What is the amount in the envelope?

Coin Riddle #4

There are 6 coins in the envelope.
Four of the coins are the same and have a double-digit value.
Two coins are each one-fourth of a dollar.
The value of all the coins is 90¢.
What coins are in the envelope?

Units versus Numbers

 Misconception

Viewing the process of measuring as a procedural counting task. For example, students count the markings on a ruler (rather than the units) resulting in an incorrect measurement of length.

What to Do

- Ask students to estimate the size of an object first before measuring it. Expect students to explain how they know their estimate is reasonable, which supports students' number sense.

- Allow students to measure real-world objects, rather than only pictures on paper. Environmental objects force children to approximate measure, a more realistic application of measurement.

- Bridge nonstandard units to standard units by providing students with manipulatives that are "standard" size (for example, one-inch color tiles, one-centimeter cubes, Cuisenaire® Rods, base-ten blocks). For example, ask students to measure the length of a pencil by lining up color tiles. Expect students to approximate the object's length first.

- Encourage students to measure the same object with a variety of nonstandard and standard units. This reinforces the importance of a unit's size, and that some units are more efficient for measuring an object.

- Allow students to make their own measuring tool, such as a ruler. This activity helps students understand a ruler's purpose, and that it's not just a tool used to complete a procedural task (see page 98).

- Provide students who are having difficulty, with rulers that have fewer markings. For example, use a ruler with only one-fourth markings (instead of one-eighth and one-sixteenth markings) to help them more clearly notice that each space (instead of a mark) on a ruler represents a unit.

- Use rulers with the "0" mark a short distance from the edge. Students will be engaged in thinking about both endpoints when measuring with this type of ruler. They will also be focusing on units (and not markings) when they measure.

- Ask students to develop and explain strategies for measuring curved and crooked lines or other hard-to-measure objects such as a door's height.

Look Fors

As students work through these activities, check for the following understandings:

- ✔ Do students understand that when units are small, more are needed to measure, and when units are large, fewer units are needed?

- ✔ Can students explain why they think their estimates are reasonable?

- ✔ Can students identify the starting point on each ruler?

Student-Made Rulers

Materials   Strips of oaktag, 2″ wide and 12″ long

Color tiles (1″ squares)

Strips of construction paper (two different colors and also a different color than color of oaktag), 1″ wide and about 15″ long

Scissors, markers, crayons, glue

Give each student a 12-inch strip of oaktag and several strips of construction paper. Students cut the construction paper strips into units using a 1″ color tile (so that each unit is one inch long). They paste the units onto their oaktag strip alternating the colors. Direct student to glue the first unit a short distance from the end. This forces students to think about where to align the units on the ruler to the object.

Note: Pasting down copies of the construction paper units on a ruler maximizes the connection between the spaces on a ruler and the actual units (Van de Walle and Lovin 2006).

■ Before students place numbers on their rulers, provide opportunities for them to use the student-made rulers to measure a variety of objects in the classroom (see literature connections on page 99). Ask them to record the measurements and to check their results by measuring the same objects with a standard ruler. Allow time for students to compare and discuss their results using both rulers. There will likely be some inaccuracies, which will make for an interesting and important discussion.

■ Finally, ask students to put numbers on their rulers. It is important to allow students to number their ruler in a way that makes sense to them! Ask student to describe why it is helpful to have numbers on a ruler.

These directions are adapted from the following resource:

Van de Walle, John, and LouAnn H. Lovin. 2006. *Teaching Student-Centered Mathematics, Grades 3–5.* Upper Saddle River, NJ: Allyn & Bacon.

Literature Connections

Hightower, Susan. 1997. *Twelve Snails to One Lizard*. New York: Simon & Schuster.

This book focuses informally on the following units of measure: twelve inches in a foot, thirty-six inches in a yard, and three feet in a yard. After reading the story, provide each student a twelve-inch strip of adding machine tape (plain with no markings). Ask them to look around the classroom to find objects that are about the same length. They can record what objects they found on their strip of paper. Then give each student a thirty-six-inch strip of adding machine tape and repeat the process. At this point, a hunt for this length can be done outside the classroom. This familiarizes students with benchmarks of one foot and one yard even though they are not formally using the standard tools.

Lionni, Leo. 1995. *Inch by Inch*. New York: HarperCollins.

After reading, students use their student-made rulers to complete the following tasks:

■ First, ask students to find an object in the classroom that is about one inch in length (without measuring). They record the predictions and check them by measuring with the student-made ruler (before numbers are placed on it). They also check their predictions by using a standard ruler. Then they list additional objects that are about an inch long.

■ Students repeat this process by making a prediction about an object in the classroom that might be about three inches. Again, they record their predictions and then measure to verify them, using the student-made rulers and a standard ruler. They then list additional objects that are about three inches.

■ Finally, ask students to predict what object in the classroom might be about six inches and measure it to verify. They record additional objects that are about six inches.

■ Allow time for students to discuss what they notice about their predictions and the actual measurements. Ask whether there were any differences in measurements between their student-made rulers and the standard ruler. If so, what may have caused the differences to occur?

Pinczes, Elinor J. 2001. *Inchworm and a Half*. Boston: Houghton-Mifflin.

It is recommended that this book be read and used when students have an understanding of half-inch units on a ruler and an understanding of the fractions ½, ⅓, and ¼. Students use their student-made rulers to measure a variety of objects. Prior to completing this task, choose objects that are six inches or less for students to measure. Also, choose several objects that are slightly longer than six inches. Ask students to think about how these objects can be measured and to also record a representation of how it was done.

Engaging Opportunities for Students

Tear off 2 strips of masking tape that are each 2 feet long. Place 1 strip in a straight line on the floor. Place the other strip in a zigzag pattern near the first strip. Ask students to make a prediction about which strip is longer. Engage students in a discussion about how to compare the strips in order to verify their prediction (for example, yarn or string, how to measure). Since the strips are the same length, students may be surprised at the results. Repeat on another day using two strips, one curved and the other zigzag. This time make 1 of the strips longer. Ask students to repeat the process by making a prediction and then discussing how to compare them to verify. Since one is longer, ask students to determine how much longer it is.

Show students a 36-inch strip of adding machine tape (or a 100-centimeter strip). Tell them they will use it to think about a reasonable estimate for the length of a classroom wall (choose a longer wall in the classroom). Allow time for students to formulate a prediction and record it on a sticky note. Facilitate a discussion about how they determined their predictions. Begin measuring the wall with the strip and stop about one-fourth along the length of the wall. Ask whether any students would like to revise their estimates and to explain why. Finally, ask students to demonstrate how to measure the wall's length using the strip (students use iteration to do this as they repeat the strip over and over). Expect students to compare the differences between their estimates and the actual measurement result. Also, since the strip is 36 inches long, ask students to figure out the length of the wall in inches. Then ask them to convert the total inches into yards.

Ask students to estimate the heights for objects that cannot be directly measured, such as the height of the wall in the classroom. Ask them to record their thinking in a journal and to explain their reasoning for why their estimate is reasonable.

Area and Perimeter

 ## Misconception

Confusing the terms *area* and *perimeter*.

What to Do

■ Allow students to explore area by covering the surface of a variety of objects with nonstandard units (for example, covering the top of a table with foam cutouts or covering the outline of a student's hand with a collection of rocks). This exercise helps them see area as the amount of surface within specific boundaries. Then move on to covering surfaces using congruent units, such as index cards or multilink cubes. Using a consistent unit allows students to compare the areas of different shapes (see page 105).

■ Connect the concepts of area and perimeter to meaningful scenarios like those in children's books. *Spaghetti and Meatballs for All!*, by Marilyn Burns, is a great story for promoting discussion. It explores how the arrangement of the same number of tables (area) impacts the amount of available seating (perimeter).

■ Give students a set amount of squares and triangles (pattern blocks work well) to use to make a tessellation. Compare the varying designs created. Compare the area of each. Discuss the notion of conservation of area. Get students to recognize that although the tessellations vary in appearance, the area is consistent for all.

■ Use a multiplication chart to illustrate the connection between the area of a rectangle and multiplicative arrays. Show students that a four-unit times

four-unit square covers an area of sixteen units. Such connections help students construct their own formulas based on their conceptual understanding rather than mimicking a formula without a context.

■ Have students use pattern blocks or square tiles to create a variety of designs with a constant perimeter. Instruct students to compare the areas of the shapes made with like materials. Discuss what trends they notice about the area of shapes that all have the same perimeter.

■ Have students shade, fold, or even cut square-grid paper to explore the relationship between area and the dimensions of length and width:

• What happens to the area of a rectangle if the length is doubled?

• How is the area affected if both the length and width are doubled? Why?

• If the length and width were cut in half, what would happen to the area?

Explorations like this reveal that doubling one dimension doubles the area, but doubling both dimensions increases the area by four times the original quantity.

■ Provide cutouts of rectangles, triangles, trapezoids, and circles and have students develop strategies for finding the area of each.

Look Fors

As students work through these activities, check for the following understandings:

✔ Do students understand that the distance around the perimeter of a figure is different from the amount of space covered by a figure?

✔ Can students cover a figure with units and count the number of units used?

✔ Are students able to see that the size of the units affects the number of units needed to measure the area or perimeter of a figure?

Name _____ Date _____

Perimeter Pictures

After listening to *Grandfather Tang's Story* by Ann Tompert, complete the steps below with your table group.

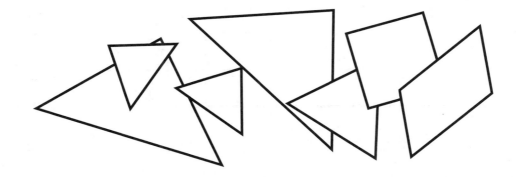

☐ Use all 7 tans to make an animal of your own. The only rule is that each tan must touch another by more than just a point.

☐ Cut out your animal.

☐ Use a ruler to measure the perimeter of your tangram animal (in centimeters).

☐ Record the perimeter on the front of your animal.

☐ With your table group, put the animals in order from the least perimeter to the greatest perimeter.

☐ Discuss the following questions with your table group:

    a. What is the area of each animal?

    b. What is the perimeter of each animal?

    c. Is there a way to predict whether a particular animal will have a larger or smaller perimeter? Why or why not?

    d. How could you rearrange your tans to make a bigger or smaller perimeter?

Name _____ Date _____

Bend and Build

Use pipe cleaners or wax sticks to form a total length of 36 centimeters. Make as many different polygons as possible with this given length on the centimeter grid paper. Label the area and perimeter of each polygon.

A = 51 square cm
P = 36 cm

Measurement: *Area and Perimeter*

Name _____ Date _____

Area and Perimeter in My World

Use a 3″ × 5″ index card as your measuring tool to estimate the area and perimeter of 6 different objects. Record a description of the object and the estimated dimensions on the table below.

Object Description	Estimated Perimeter	Estimated Area
1.		
2.		
3.		
4.		
5.		
6.		

Explain your strategy for estimating perimeter.

Explain your strategy for estimating area.

Conversions

 Misconception

When adding or subtracting with different units of measure students rename with units of ten or regroup with units of ten, just as they do when they rename or regroup with whole numbers. For example, when comparing 3′2″ to 1′7″ a student may incorrectly rename 3′2″ as 2′12″ as they would when subtracting with tens and ones.

What to Do

■ Give students time to explore with whatever units of measure are being used, prior to giving students problems to solve (whether they be story problems or numerical expressions).

■ Have students record different ways to represent the same unit of measure. (For example: 1 hour is the same as 60 minutes and 0 seconds, 1 hour is the same as 59 minutes and 60 seconds, 1 hour is the same as 58 minutes and 120 seconds . . .).

■ Have students discuss what they might have to do if they want to know what the difference would be between two units of measure when subtracting involves renaming. (For example: What if you had 2 hours before your bedtime? You watch a television program and 2 commercials and see that 37 minutes have passed. How will you figure out exactly how much time you have left to stay up?) Have students share their ideas for solving a story problem like this and then discuss whether these answers make sense; try them out with units of linear measure, liquid measure, and time.

Look Fors

✔ Look to see that students represent addition and subtraction of time, length, or fractions with the appropriate conversions.

✔ Have students use illustrations, whenever possible, to represent different ways to name the same thing.

✔ Provide students with manipulative materials to represent fractions in multiple ways.

Name _____ Date _____

Figuring Out Different Ways to Show Liquid Measure

Read the story problem below and use whatever you need to use to help you get answers to this problem. You may draw pictures, use symbols, or write to explain your thinking.

Cassie needs to make 640 ounces of lemonade, which will be brought to the campgrounds for campers to drink. She only has 1 one-gallon container and 3 one-quart containers, but plenty of one-cup and one-pint containers for preparing and delivering the lemonade. What are 5 *different* ways she could use these containers to make and transport this amount of lemonade?

Name _____ Date _____

Happy Thanksgiving: A Problem with Cooking

The whole family is involved in preparing the Thanksgiving turkey! At the local supermarket, $.79 a pound is a real bargain. There will be 15 guests for dinner and we are told to allow for at least ¾ of a pound to 1 pound of turkey per guest. A 20-pound bird is bought—just in case.

The cookbook calls for the turkey to cook at 350 degrees for 25 minutes per pound. If dinner will be served at 6:30 p.m. at what time does the turkey need to be put into the oven so that it is finished cooking at 6:00 p.m.? (It needs to cool a bit before being carved.)

Use pictures, words, and symbols to figure out the answer to this problem. When you are finished you may also want to determine the cost of the turkey.

Illustrate, Compute, Explain

Use **I. C. E.** to solve this story problem.

Tanisha is making headbands to sell for a fund-raiser given by her youth group. Each headband needs 7 inches of fabric. She buys 1 yard of fabric from the store and makes a headband right away. How much fabric does she have left?

Illustrate / **C**ompute

Explain:

_____

_____

_____

_____

Measurement: *Conversions*

Sorting and Classifying

 ## Misconception

Misunderstanding the meaning of vocabulary associated with sorting and organizing data because of limited experiences in completing these tasks.

What to Do

- Reinforce language used in organizing, describing, and analyzing data (for example, *not, all, some, not equal, most, fewer, similar, in common, predict, always*).

- Let students work with attribute blocks, which are a *structured* sorting material with easily identifiable characteristics (see page 111).

- Allow children to name a "mystery" sorting rule based on clues given to them. Students apply reasoning and logic as they eliminate possible sorting rules (see page 111). Model language mentioned in first bullet.

- Let students sort three-dimensional shapes to reinforce geometric vocabulary in addition to sorting vocabulary.

- Provide a variety of *unstructured* materials as well for sorting and classifying. Because unstructured materials have many different attributes and possibilities for sorting, they can be more challenging to describe and classify. Unstructured materials include, for example, seashells, buttons, or canceled postage stamps (for example, sorting international stamps by countries or by continents). Expect student to describe sorts using language mentioned in first bullet.

- Ask each student to create a triangle on a geoboard using one rubber band. Let students sort triangles as a whole class first. Possibilities: size, type of angles (right, acute, obtuse), type of triangle (equilateral, isosceles, scalene), or number of pegs inside triangles (fewer than four pegs, four or more pegs). Ask students to make additional triangles on geoboard recording sheets (see page 112). Partners sort combined triangles two different ways. The triple Venn diagram on page 113 can be used for sorting.

- Ask students to sort collected data, organize them, and represent them in two different displays. Students describe both ways the data were organized. Ask them to choose the most appropriate display and to justify why it is an efficient way to communicate the information.

- Let small groups of students sort about thirty buttons into a triple Venn diagram. Challenge students to think of several ways to sort buttons.

Look Fors

As students work through these activities, check for the following understandings:

- ✔ Do students understand the language of "not" (for example, "Not a button with four holes.") when determining sorts? Are they able to use terms such as *some* and *predict*?

- ✔ Are students able to determine multiple sorting rules for objects?

- ✔ Do students apply reasoning in making decisions about sorting and classifying?

Attribute Block Tasks

Attribute blocks are considered *structured* materials because their attributes are easily identified and described by students. These blocks allow students to focus on the reasoning skills necessary to complete tasks with the blocks. Attribute blocks have 4 distinct attributes: shape (rectangle, square, triangle, hexagon, and circle), size (large and small), color (red, yellow, and blue), and thickness (thin and thick). Several tasks that support students' abilities to describe attributes, sort, and think logically follow:

- Exploration. Allow students to first explore attribute blocks before completing any tasks. In a whole-group discussion, ask students to tell what they noticed about the blocks when they were exploring them. Record their descriptions on chart paper. For example, if a student says the blocks are different colors, begin a list of the colors for the attribute blocks.

- How Long Can We Make It? Arrange students in a circle on the floor. Place an attribute block in the center so that all can see it easily. Ask students to describe its attributes. Then place another block next to it that is different in only 1 way. For example, a thick, large yellow hexagon is placed next to a thin, large yellow hexagon. These blocks are only different in 1 way: thickness. Challenge students to figure out what block could be next and to state how they know it goes next. A thin, large yellow square could go next, which is different only by shape. Students continue to place blocks until no more blocks can be placed. Students are focusing on attributes and explaining their reasoning in their choice of blocks. Later, ask student to arrange blocks by connecting those that are different in 2 different ways each time.

- Yes or No? Record 2 sorting rules on 5″ × 7″ index cards (for example, "small, thick shapes" and "not red"). Overlap 2 hoops on the floor in front of students. Turn index cards upside down on each hoop. Tell students you will respond either "yes" or "no" as they choose shapes to place inside the hoops. Expect students to explain their reasoning in choosing shapes to place in the hoops. After students have chosen about 7 to 10 shapes, they will notice commonalities that the shapes share in the different parts of the double-Venn diagram (some shapes will be outside the hoops). Ask students to predict what the mystery rules are and to explain their reasoning for how they know this. Challenge students to solve a triple-Venn diagram with mystery rules (for example, large 4-sided shapes; not thick; thin).

Geoboard Recording Sheet for Triangle Sorting Task

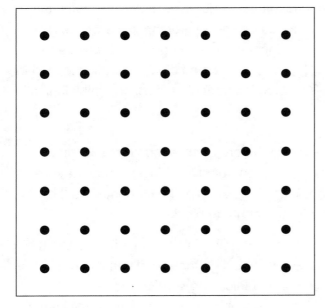

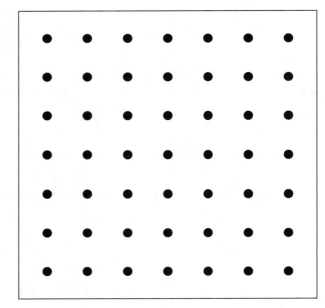

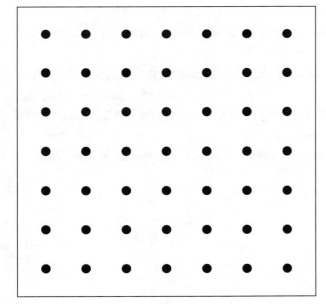

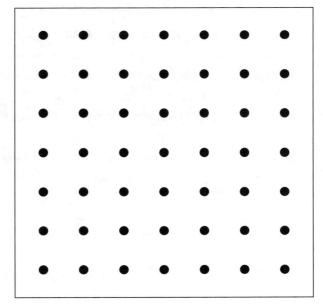

Data Analysis and Probability: *Sorting and Classifying*

Name _____   Date _____

Triple Venn Diagram

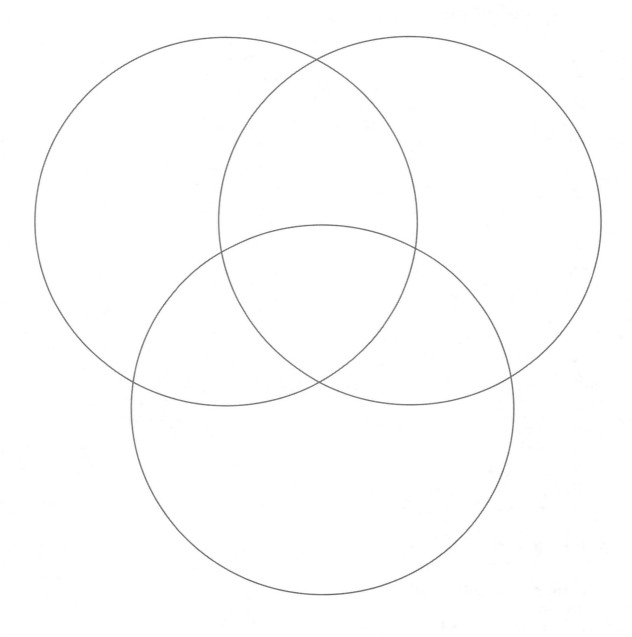

Choosing an Appropriate Display

Misconception

Any type of display can be used for a set of data.

What to Do

- Make the data collection and analysis process meaningful by helping students first identify the question they wish to answer. Formulating the question provides direction in the collection and representation stages. Rather than graphing favorite ice cream flavors or class birthdays simply for the sake of making a graph, create a purposeful question the graph is meant to answer. Students will learn the parts of a graph and how to put the pieces together, with intent and purpose. Possible questions include:

  - How will we know when someone in our class is celebrating a birthday?

  - How can we keep track of how everyone gets home from school in the afternoon?

  - What types of books should be purchased for the library?

  - Where in the room is the best place for our plants to grow?

- Provide examples of both numerical and categorical data so students will be more likely to understand why certain data displays are more appropriate than others. (Numerical examples include age, shoe size, height, money earned; categorical examples include kinds of pets, movie types, foods, names.)

- Ask students to collect graphs from newspapers, magazines, and websites. Sort the examples according to types. Allow students to speculate why a specific graph was used to represent the data and why another representation would not work as well to convey the information.

- Create two different displays for a given set of data (see page 116). Ask students to compare the two displays and discuss whether they carry the same message. This activity will help students see that the kind of graph they choose can impact the visual message. (One way to do this is by using connecting cubes to represent the bars on a bar graph. Students can then replicate the quantity of each color and arrange them in a circle to see how the same data would look as a circle graph.)

- Make large versions of graphs as a class (an easy way is to use a shower curtain liner and traffic tape). These visual aids enhance class discussions about the parts of a graph and the most appropriate way to display the data.

- Gather a collection of graph templates to which students can refer. These visual prompts can help students compare the potential final product and help connect the data to a potential display.

Look Fors

As students work through these activities, check for the following understandings:

- ✔ Can students recall the question being answered through the collection and display process?

- ✔ Do students understand the parts of each type of data display appropriate for their grade level?

- ✔ Can students compare the attributes of different types of displays?

Data Display Decisions

Which type of graph would be the best way to display the data?
Explain why for each choice.

	Bar graph	**Line graph**	**Line plot**

1. The favorite color of the students in your class   _____

2. The age of each president when he took office   _____

3. The daily temperature for 1 month   _____

4. Most rented movies   _____

5. The number of home runs in a season   _____

6. Minutes each student reads each week   _____

What's the Same? What's Different?

Look at the 2 graphs below. Tell a friend how they are alike and how they are different.

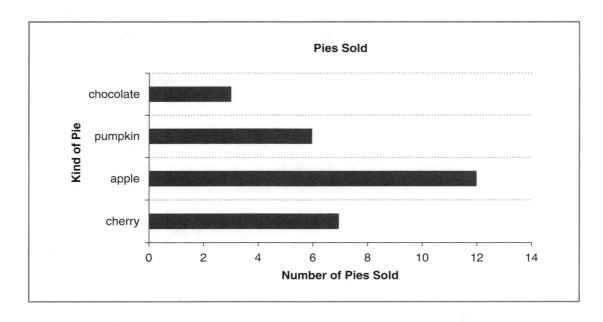

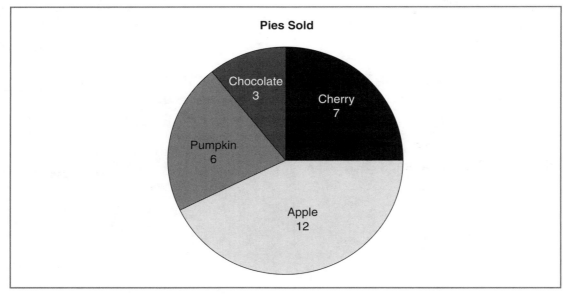

Name _____ Date _____

Collecting and Displaying Data for a Purpose

Choose a question to be answered by collecting data and then conduct a survey to gather the data. Show the data using an appropriate display:

- ■ Bar graph

- ■ Circle graph

- ■ Line graph

- ■ Line plot

- ■ Stem and leaf plot

- ■ Pictograph

Consider how these data might be used and share your work with the class.

Mean, Median, and Mode

 ## Misconception

Determining the middle of a set of data (to find the median) without sequencing the data from least to most or most to least. Determining the mode by finding the greatest amount in a set of data. Determining the median without using the number of zeroes in the set.

What to Do

- Whenever possible link concrete experiences to the procedures that students will be using to determine mean, median, and mode.

- Provide students with opportunities to define the terms they're learning about once these have been talked about.

- Provide students with many opportunities to collect and then summarize their own data so they have a clear sense of the concepts of each of these levels of central tendency.

- Have students experience a variety of problem types so they develop a truer sense of what each measure of central tendency measures.

- For students to better understand the impact that zero has on determining the mean it helps to have them construct different data sets, for a specific mean, where zero has to be included.

Look Fors

As students work through these activities, check for the following understandings:

- ✔ As students collect data look and listen to how they decide to organize this information as they determine the mean, median, and mode.

- ✔ As students explain how the mean was determined, look to see if they had zero in their data set. If they did not, ask them what would happen if zero was in the set.

- ✔ See if students can tell you when this sort of data would be used, by whom, and for what purpose.

Name _____ Date _____

Chocolate Chip Cookie Problem

The 26 fifth graders in Ms. Reynolds' class made a line plot to represent how many chocolate chips each student had in the chocolate chip cookie each was given. Here is their line plot.

How Many Chocolate Chips Did We Have in Our Cookies?

```
                                        X
                                        X
                        X           X   X
                    X   X           X   X           X
                X   X   X           X   X   X   X
        X       X   X   X           X   X   X   X           X
        _____
        0   1   2   3   4   5   6   7   8   9   10  11
```

Figure out the mean, median, and mode of the class' data and explain how you figured out each.

Candy Averages

Emily buys a large bag of candies. She eats some candy nearly every day for 2 weeks. On average she eats 12 candies each day. Create a data set to show how many candies she eats during this 2-week period. There must be at least 1 day when she doesn't eat any candy.

Decide whether the average you are finding is the mean, median, or mode and explain why you've chosen this average.

Data Analysis and Probability: *Mean, Median, and Mode*

Name _____ Date _____

Links in a Minute

You will have 1 minute to connect as many links as possible. Before you begin, estimate how many links you think you will be able to connect in 1 minute.

I predict that I will be able to connect _____ links in a minute.

Now you will be timed for 1 minute. You may begin when your teacher says "start."

I was able to connect _____ links in a minute.
The difference between these amounts is _____.

When we put ourselves in order from the fewest links connected to the most links connected, the fewest was _____ and the most was _____.

The range for this data was _____.

To figure out whether there was a mode we _____

_____

_____

_____

The mode was _____.

To figure out the median we _____

_____

_____

_____

The median was _____.

To figure out the mean we _____

_____

_____

_____

The mean was _____.

Data Analysis and Probability: *Mean, Median, and Mode*

Analyzing Data

 Misconception

Incorrectly analyzing the data on a graph.

What to Do

■ Use color to distinguish different categories of data on a graph (different-color connecting cubes or links when creating a graph with manipulatives, multicolored crayons or markers when constructing graphs on paper). Color variations allow students to more readily compare and contrast the data.

■ Designate a space in the classroom in which to display a variety of tables and graphs. Encourage students to collect examples as well. Make a daily data chat part of the morning routine. Ask students to share what the data show, and brainstorm who might be interested in such information.

■ Ask students to describe the shape of data—the visual image conveyed by a graph. Provide graphed data minus the titles and labels. Ask students to describe the trend they see and name some possible titles and labels based on those trends. Or conduct this activity as a matching game: titles and labels on one set of cards, graphed data on another. Have students match the data to the correct title and labels.

■ Give students different-size representations of the same data. (Modifications might include changing the scale or the length of the axis.) Ask them to consider what is revealed by the different perspectives. Examples like these prompt rich discussions of comparisons and visual messages. Helping stu-

dents realize how choices with regard to the axes and the scales influence the appearance of the data will help learners be more critical in their data analysis.

■ Use technology to expose students to multiple views of the same data. Many software applications allow students to input quantities and then choose from a variety of displays. With the click of the mouse, students can see the data transformed from a bar graph to a circle graph. By comparing the data as represented on different types of graphs, students can decide which provides a clearer picture of their intent. If students choose an incorrect display (for example, turn a pie chart into a line graph) you can ask about the validity of the data and the appropriateness of the graph given the data set.

Look Fors

As students work through these activities, check for the following understandings:

✔ Can students link the data points to the display to explain why the graph looks the way it does?

✔ Are students able to explain the graph to others?

✔ Can students describe how a graph might change if there were a change in the data?

Graph Scavenger Hunt

Search for a graph (newspaper, magazine, Internet) and glue it in the space below. Write the story the graph tells.

Data Analysis and Probability: *Analyzing Data*

Name _____ Date _____

What Do We Now Know?

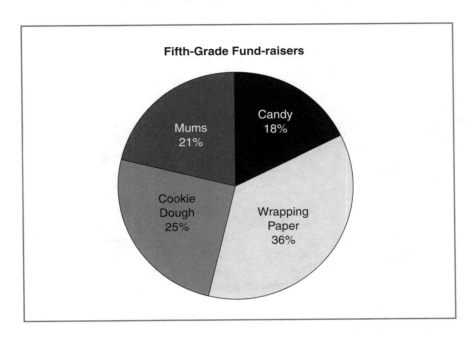

Write 3 questions that could be answered using the circle graph above:

1.

2.

3.

Painting a Different Picture

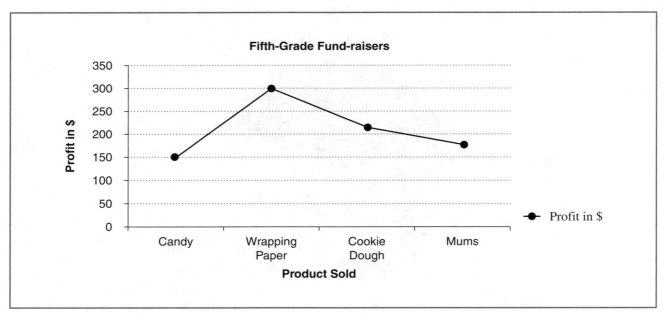

What is wrong with the data display above?

How could the graph be changed to correctly display the data?

Data Analysis and Probability: *Analyzing Data*

What Does "Fair" Mean?

 Misconception

Believing that factors other than having an equally likely opportunity to win make a game or activity fair.

What to Do

- Use spinners split into different parts (some halves, some fourths, some sixths, and some eighths) and use only two colors to color these parts. For the fourths show ¾ of one color and only ¼ of the other color. For the sixths, show ⁴⁄₆ one color and ²⁄₆ of the other color. For the eighths show ³⁄₈ of one color and ⁵⁄₈ of the other color. Have students play in pairs and assign one color to one student and the other color to the other student. Have students record what happens when each spins the same amount of times. Then discuss whether one person has a greater chance of getting one color over the other, and why this is so.

- Use different sorts of dice (hexahedron, octahedron, decahedron) and have students play in pairs (see page 128). One student gets a point if the number is even, the other gets a point if the number is odd. Have students toss the dice and keep track of their points. Then discuss whether the activity is fair. Does each person have an equally likely chance of getting a point?

- Use different sorts of dice (hexahedron, octahedron, decahedron) and have four students playing together. One student gets a point if the outcome of a toss is even. One gets a point if the outcome of a toss is odd. One gets a point if the outcome of a toss is a square number. One gets a point if the outcome of a toss is a prime number. Have students keep track of their points and the number of times the die is tossed. Discuss the fairness of this game. Does one person have a better chance of winning than another?

- Place 10 colored cubes—5 yellow, 4 red, and 1 green—in an opaque bag. Have students work in pairs and pull out a cube, record the color, and then replace it in the bag. Have students do this for 25 pulls. Discuss the outcomes of this experiment as a class. Is it likely for each color to be pulled out the same amount of times?

Look Fors

As students work through these activities, check for the following understandings:

✔ Fairness involves having an equally likely opportunity to be spun, picked, or worn.

✔ Just because an activity is fun does not mean that it is a fair activity.

✔ If there are more of one thing than another it is likely that the greater amount will make the activity unfair.

Name _____ Date _____

What Makes a Game Fair?

Before beginning this activity decide who will be Player 1 and who will be Player 2.

Player 1: _____

Player 2: _____

You have 2 decahedron die that will be tossed. Player 1 gets a point if the *product* of the 2 die is **even**. Player 2 gets a point if the *product* of the 2 die is **odd**. Talk about whether you think this will be a "fair" game given these directions. Explain in writing what makes this fair or unfair.

_____

_____

_____

_____

_____

_____

_____

_____

_____

Then, decide on a way to keep track of your tosses and do this experiment for 25 tosses. Look at your data and compare what you thought would happen with what actually happened.

Be prepared to share your observations and your ideas about what happened.

Name _____ Date _____

Which Sum Will Appear Most Often?

Use 2 fair numeral cubes to do this experiment. Before tossing the cubes write out all of the possible sums that can be created.

POSSIBLE SUMS:

Which sum do you think you will get the most if you toss these 2 cubes? _____

What makes you think that this sum will appear most often?

_____

_____

Begin tossing the cubes and recording the sum that you got. When time is up figure out how many of each sum you got. Create a line plot to show these sums.

Sums Recorded

Line Plot to Show My Results

May be copied for classroom use. © 2010 by Honi J. Bamberger and Christine Oberdorf from *Activities to Undo Math Misconceptions*, *Grades 3–5* (Heinemann: Portsmouth, NH).

Name _____ Date _____

Making Sense of Probability Vocabulary

Directions: Complete each sentence and illustrate what you've written about.

I am **certain** that

It is **highly likely** that

It is **highly unlikely** that

It is **impossible** that

Data Analysis and Probability: *What Does "Fair" Mean?*

Spinners for "Spinning for Sums or Differences" Activity (page 8)

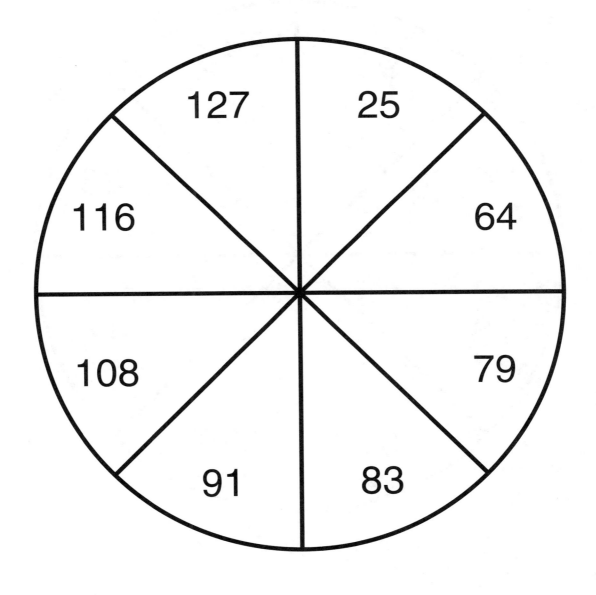

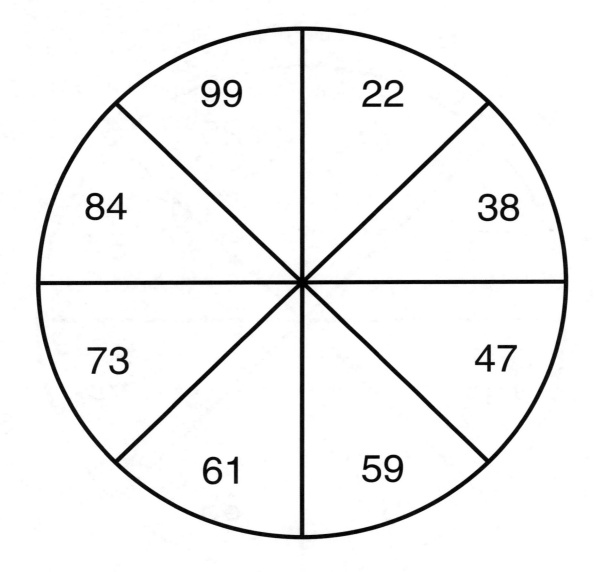

Spinner for "Equal Groupings" Activity (page 16)

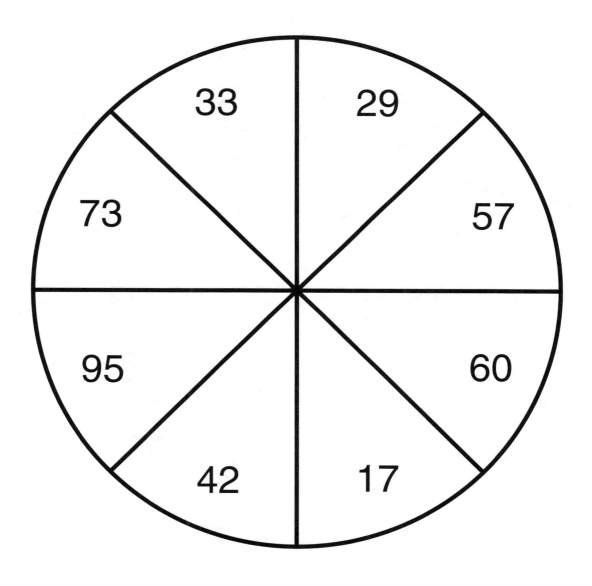

Appendix C

Spinner for "Pathways" Activity (page 42)

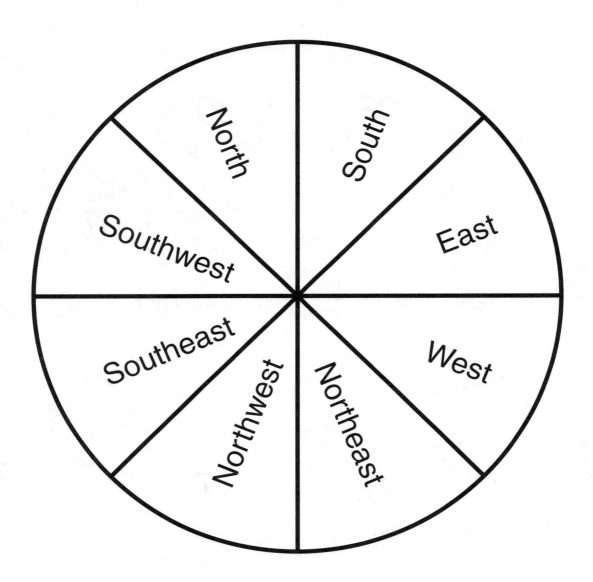